SECRETS

FAMILY, FRIENDS, AND MENTAL ILLNESS

Diana L. Dodds BSN

Secrets/ Diana Dodds. -- 1st ed.

ISBN 978-1-7328099-0-1

LCCN 201 8911720

Contents

Dedicated with love and great appreciation to my loving husband, Mark, and my children, Patrick and Jacob, whose support has made this book possible.

To Roger, Diane, Joline, Naida, Thomas, Victoria, Andrea, Janna, Mary Anne, Cami, Betty, and Laura, my colleagues in memoir writing who patiently listened to my writing along the way, and shared their expertise.

To Dr. Judith Milner who always believed that I had a story to tell and the ability to tell it.

PREFACE

From time to time, if we are fortunate, we have an epiphany. This ability to have an insight into the circumstances of our life has the potential to cause a major shift in its trajectory. Just to have insight is often not significant enough on its own, because there needs to be the support to follow through with that change. Knowledge is a catalyst, and it is often lacking in families when the subject is mental illness.

The percentage of people who will have major mental illness in their lifetime, quoted at this time, is 20%, or 1 out of every 5 people. With numbers like that, it is reasonable to assume that no family, no matter how influential, can say that there is no mental illness in their family. There very well could be mentally ill individuals that are denied by those families or whose history is hidden, but they exist.

Our country's history has shown that there was a belief that mental illness was a character flaw or a genetic weakness that could be eliminated, or if not eliminated, then hidden. The term "fit" became a term to be desired in relationship to parents and children and their ancestry.

The mystery exists in every family at one level or another. The possibility of finding ways to advance the treatment and perhaps someday find a cure for mental illness will depend on those self-same families being willing to leave the darkness and step into the light. The past holds the key to the future.

CHAPTER ONE

HOW DID I GET HERE?

Sun streamed through the lower third of the tall windows behind the nurse's station. The station stood as a bastion of reason overlooking the large activity room on the psychiatric unit. The activity room was the center of the floor with three rays jutting out from there which held patient rooms. I sat at a small wooden table towards the back of the room and leafed through a book, and stared at the shiny linoleum floor.

The elevator doors just up the hall from the activity room opened and a tall red-haired woman stepped out in a conservative grey dress and heels, followed by four young women in blue uniforms with white pinafore-like fronts and white nursing caps. I dropped down lower in the overstuffed chair I was in and lifted the book over my face until they passed. I peeked over the top of the book as the young ladies walked behind the woman, like so many ducklings, into the safety of the nurse's station. They began picking up charts and pulling papers out of their pockets. I knew what they were doing. They were preparing for their next day of school.

My experience told me that this was going to be a deep dive into each patient's life for those assigned to these students. They would be looking at family history. Were there any alcoholics, suicides, diagnosed mentally-ill members of the immediate or extended family? Had this person had any previous hospitalizations? What was this person's home life like? What was the inciting incident that had them hospitalized this time? Just like students always looked at histories and physicals, lab work, diagnostic exams, and medications and then correlated them all for physical illness, they would be looking at all the information that most people kept to themselves and hoped never to reveal. Was one of those charts they were laboring over mine? What would they think of me, a nurse who had just had a psychotic break? How would I ever face one of those young women in the future should we meet in a professional situation? What if there was no future for me?

Quietly, the stately woman from the elevator nearly glided to my table. I felt a rush of heat rising from my chest to my cheeks. I tried so hard not to look into her eyes, and glanced away.

"Diana, I just have a few moments, but I wanted to assure you that the students would not have access to your chart. The nurses will not use your name in report, so you don't need to worry."

"Thank you. That relieves my mind."

"How are you managing?"

"I'm bored right now. There isn't much to do when you aren't meeting with the doctor or visiting with your husband. I was trying to read something, but my vision has been changed with the anti-psychotics that I'm on."

"Ah, side effects."

"If I hold the book as far away from me as I can, I can see, but it's too far away to read. I bring it closer and everything blurs."

"I'm sorry about that. Maybe they'll be able to change the medicine eventually. The other instructors wanted me to tell you that they hope you feel better soon."

"That's kind of them."

"I have to go for now, but we will be up on the floor tomorrow," she said with a genuine smile.

Part of me was relieved that the students wouldn't be able to read about my psychotic break, but part of me felt terrible sadness that I couldn't join in with them. I loved teaching students. Would I ever be able to work as a nurse again? What would my life be after this? I began to ponder what in my past might have caused my mind to crumble. I felt a need to understand the cause. Perhaps I could prevent it in the future.

When I had been in psychiatric nursing classes in school, the teachers cautioned us not to indulge in hypochondria. There were times that I was sure that the symptoms of one disease or another fit me or my family, but then I would laugh it off. Now, I had to reconsider it. We had been instructed on the power of environment to cause mental illness. At this point, however, I wasn't even sure what illness I suffered from. 'How did I get here?' was what kept playing on the tape in my mind.

CHAPTER TWO

THE OPENING VOLLEY

The summer of 1961 was in full swing. The sky was like an artist's palette of pale blues and faint yellows interrupted with scattered fluffy clouds.

"Diana, it's time to go to the farm," Mom called as she stepped out onto the covered cement porch of our house in Goodland, Kansas. Our Sunday ritual always began with a trip to Grandma Middleton's farm. For Dad, this farm was home, and on these excursions he seemed to imagine himself one day having a piece of it. Every Sunday, he worked on his cars in Grandma's large garage, while we played around on the property. There were a few cars of his, like a 56 Ford Fairlane and a 32 Chevy Coup, that he left parked on the farm like flags on a new shore.

I climbed into the back seat of our gold and white 58 Chevy with my oldest sister, Cheryl. Cheryl was 4 years my senior at eleven years of age. Her brunette waves surrounded her stormy face. She heaved a heavy sigh as the car backed out of the driveway. She had lived her first 6 years on the farm, and had other places she would rather be. With my parents up front, we headed out of town. As we turned onto Highway 24, I watched familiar flat land become low rolling hills with fields of wheat, here and there interspersed with fallow ground.

After about fifteen minutes, the car took a left turn and lurched up a steep hill on a gravel drive to the front of my grandmother's turquoise house. Surrounded by a white picket fence, it was flanked by scattered juniper bushes, a row of juniper trees, flowers, and a small patch of Kentucky blue grass. The yard looked well cared for and welcoming.

Within seconds of the car stopping, my tennis shoes made a scraping sound as I gathered traction on the gravel. Grandma's garden beckoned only yards away. The gate squeaked as I opened it and then I let it slam behind me, bam. Along the fence, the lush strawberry plants extended for row upon row. I paused to paw through the green leaves for the red, plump strawberries hiding beneath. Grabbing one up, I thrust it into my mouth and warm juice dripped down my chin. The strawberries were sweet and tart, and I sat on the ground for a few minutes to eat my fill, entirely forgetting to go to the house to say hello to Grandma.

At seven years of age, I often sought out such quiet scenes. Here, I could be free of the clamor and eruptions that were a constant in my home fourteen miles away. Outside, I could run and climb and pretend whatever I desired and escape from that world. My imaginary world had heroes and villains, but I could make them do whatever I pleased. In my real life, so much was outside of my control. Sundays for me meant open spaces, warm sun on my face, and freedom to be a child in the country.

Out the garden gate again, I ran past two dwarf cherry trees and passed the short buffalo grass, which sprouted up from the light brown soil. In the distance, I heard the slow squeaking of the rusty metal blades of the windmill and headed in that direction. From the windmill, I ran into the cool, taller carpet of grass at the base of the wooden water storage tower. A rivulet flowed from the overflow of the windmill's tank. Off came my shoes as I stepped in the mud and felt it ooze between my toes. My feet made a sucking sound as I lifted them, and I smiled to myself. I relished these moments.

Running through the grass, I was able to clear off the mud as I ran down a gentle slope to a large mulberry tree. The branches spread out gracefully and made it an easy climb onto the rough bark of the first large branch, which hid me behind waving green leaves. The air was so fresh, clean, and warm, and I could see the glint of the sun. The light-gold wheat field a few feet from the tree went on as far as the eye could see. Waves like the ocean coursed through the rows and rows of flowing wheat. I could hear the wheat rustling in response to the breeze.

"Hey, we're making boats up in the garage," my younger cousin shouted to me. He had followed me down the hill. I smiled at him. Four of my other cousins had arrived at the house and were going toward the garage. Scurrying down the branch, I joined him and we both ran full tilt to join the other cousins.

The old cement building smelled of oil and old grease. A car sat over a pit in the floor, where my father worked on it from below. My sister, Cheryl, was sitting on the cold cement floor cleaning engine parts for Dad, without so much as a 'Good job' or 'Thanks for helping'. She would do whatever she had to do just for some attention from him. She was Daddy's girl.

My attention was drawn quickly to my cousins who were already rifling through pieces of wood scraps, nails, various metal washers, and screws. I joined in, pounding bits together. In a few minutes, I held mine up to examine it. One silver screw served as a turret and another was the command tower.

"Meet you at the cow trough," an older cousin shouted and ran ahead of the rest of us. Like a herd of cows stampeding, we sprinted across from the garage to a tall wooden fence. The water trough on the other side of the fence became the site for a full-scale naval engagement, as six of us cousins, ranging from six to fifteen, began motoring our boats in the smelly brown water. Neither the smell nor the color of the water deterred us, though. Fantasy was in charge. I joined in the fun with my imaginary destroyer. Soon, we were all wet and laughing.

"You kids get washed up, it's supper time," Grandma Middleton bellowed from the house, while she rang a large brass bell that startled us from our reverie. Grandma was short and stocky, and she shifted her weight back and forth from one leg to another as she walked. Her hip had been broken years ago after being kicked by a cow. It didn't heal right, because they couldn't afford a doctor, and she had to keep cooking for a family with 6 kids, her husband's uncle, and of course her husband. She worked her way around the kitchen at that time keeping one leg on a chair as she moved, according to my mom. When she carried a bucket of milk, she carried a bucket of sand in the other hand to keep her balanced. This gait she had developed was the result. She had worked hard her whole life. In spite of that, her face was soft and round, with a broad smile and wispy light brown and gray hair that was gathered up in a net to hide how thin it had become. She was about five foot three inches tall, and wore heavy support hose rolled down below her knees as well as orthopedic shoes. She always had a hug waiting for any one of us who wanted it.

Hot dogs on buns, chips from a bag, and a glass of milk were our usual Sunday fare. With so many people to feed, Grandma kept it simple. Besides my cousins, my family, and me, four of my aunts and uncles joined us in the Sunday repast.

Aunt Marie, my father's oldest sister, was a gentle soul. She looked a lot like her mother but taller, with light blue eyes and the same fine light brown hair also gathered up in a net. She could easily get lost in her noisy family. I kept my eye on her because she often ended up at the upright piano in the family room, and I much preferred her music to the adult chatter.

This Sunday, Marie ate quickly and I plunked myself down next to her and paced myself along with her. No one seemed to notice either one of us, and that was fine with me. It was good to be invisible sometimes, and I knew Marie liked being invisible, too. After she finished eating, she went into the family room at the back of the house and sat down at the piano. I quickly took my plate into the kitchen and followed her. Marie could play music as she remembered it in her mind. "Playing by ear" was what they called it. I found it amazing that she could just hear a song and play it back with such confidence. She loved to play hymns that she knew. I didn't know all of the old hymns, but when she broke into "How Great Thou Art" I jumped up next to her and belted it out the best I could. We reveled in the music and I felt her joy, which I saw in her so seldom.

Religion was a centerpiece of both of my parents' upbringings, and I had attended church since I was two weeks old. Grandma Alma was a staunch Methodist. When she heard us singing hymns, she made her way into the room and seated herself on the couch. Marie was playing one of her favorite hymns, "Rock of Ages". When we finished, Grandma started making requests.

Out in the dining room, the adults were chattering amongst themselves, while the rest of the kids played out in the old closed-in porch. With music in our ears,

Marie and I could only hear snippets of the conversation.

"Did you hear what Marie said about that minister?" one aunt broke into the conversation.

"What has she said about that now?" her husband inquired.

"Something about him propositioning her up in the choir loft," another uncle chimed in. "She swore he talked into her ear while she was singing." The rest of the group joined in the laughter.

"She was probably hearing voices," he added. The others chuckled at the thought. I didn't like it when they laughed at Marie.

"Well, that pastor did run off with another woman from that church," my mom said defensively, looking toward the family room to check for a response, but Marie just continued to play.

I closed my eyes and tried to will my aunts and uncles to change the subject.

My oldest uncle must have received my unspoken message. "Did you hear that my friend from Colorado is coming out next week? We're going to go look at a steam locomotive together. We might go in as partners on it," he said. The conversation continued from there.

After dinner, everyone dispersed, some to visit in small pairings, others to do tasks around the farm. Before long, the sun went down. Dad finished working on his car for the day, and it was time for my immediate family to go home.

We piled into our Chevy. I rested my head against the back window to stare up at the sky while one after another points of light appeared.

"Virgil, they were laughing at Marie behind her back. Why do they always do that to her?" Mom asked my dad in hushed tones. She hated anyone ridiculing another person. She had not been raised that way.

Dad lit a cigarette and cracked open the window to flick ashes out. I could see his eyes in the rearview mirror, and the disgusted scowl on his face. "Well, they call me crazy, don't they?" I knew that he was always on Marie's side on most things, because the family did the same kind of thing to him.

Dad's extended family could be like wolves looking for a weakness in their pack. One false move, and you could be the one under attack. I felt that Grandma loved me, but I wondered if her love was conditional. Keeping your weaknesses to yourself seemed like the smart thing to do.

CHAPTER THREE

MIDDLETON FAMILY NIGHT

Years came and went, and by the time I was twelve years of age, the freedom to play and imagine as I had done when I was younger was gone. I hated the idea of growing up, because inside I still wanted the escape of imaginative play, but life at my home required me to be serious. I had to pay attention and watch out for Dad's moods.

I did have a new way to transport myself to that calm and stable world: through music. One evening, sitting cross-legged on the floor, I was listening to the Beatles on the stereo and singing along, when the old white Dodge drove up out front and screeched to a stop, followed by the car door slamming. Dad was home from his job as a meter reader for the city. His heavy footfalls came up the porch to the door at the side of the house. What mood would he be in? Each encounter with Dad was like approaching a minefield until I could discern which version of him I would be meeting this time.

Dad, in a good mood, could tell great stories or make up words to songs on the radio and make us all laugh. He could hold us spellbound with his exploits growing up during the Depression. Or he could be volatile, dark, and scary. There was no way to know, though I watched his face and body language carefully for cues.

Dad walked in the door and—bang!—it closed hard behind him. Slamming doors was never a good sign. I scrambled to turn off the stereo. In a bad mood, Dad hated to have music playing unless it was Benny Goodman.

"Shut off that damn noise. How can you listen to that shit?" He threw his meter book whizzing across the room and it banged against the wall. I knew it was time to make myself as small a target as possible, and stay out of sight. His verbal assaults could be brutal. As Dad ranted around the house, my two sisters, Cheryl, 16, and my four-year-old sister, Chris, retreated to their rooms. My mother would try to placate him, which really seemed to do just the opposite. He was full of rage, and there was no real way to know what the trigger had been this time. I carefully followed behind him as he stomped into the kitchen. The drama was mounting and I wanted to try to run interference for my mother if she needed help.

"I wouldn't have to put up with this God damn shit if I had the farm!" Dad screamed. He hated his job as a meter reader. Actually, he had hated every job he had ever done in town, because he felt that he had been forced off of the farm by my grandma and her eldest son, Mike.

"I'm going out there to shoot their heads off."

"Oh, Virgil, don't do that," Mom pleaded. From my corner of the room I looked from Dad to Mom and back again. Mom had learned enough over the years not to be confrontational with him, because it just escalated his behavior. She had told me that she feared he might think that he had to prove something, and she couldn't take the chance.

"Why in the hell couldn't my mom treat me like your mom treated you?"

"I don't know, Virgil. It's not right." I could feel her wanting to comfort him and try to reduce his rage, and yet she kept her distance.

"You are God damn right. Your parents loved you and they wouldn't have treated you like I've been treated. Those God damn sons-a-bitches," he said. I wondered if my mother felt guilty for her good fortune.

I'd seen this back and forth between my parents go on for hours at a time. My mother would listen and try to comfort Dad as she became a punching bag to his torrent of hateful words about nearly everyone in his life. Mother's family had been quiet, gentle people, and Dad's cursing still made her wince. Her parents had embraced my father when they had married, and he had been invited to move to Perry, Iowa, where they lived, but Dad wouldn't do it. My grandfather Kibby, Mom's father, had offered to teach him to be a tool and die maker which would have been a good living, but this was not the future he wanted.

The farm was Dad's quest. My grandmother Middleton had six children, but only one child, her oldest, Mike, would receive any of the farm when she died, or work it while she was alive as far as she was concerned. My father's crusade was more about being seen as an equal to his brother than about love of land. Land could be bought or rented if farming was what he really wanted to do, but if it wasn't the land he grew up on, then it didn't count for shit. Dad's father had told him that he was meant to be a farmer, but had died and left the farm in Grandma Middleton's hands. And that left Dad feeling as if he were out in the cold.

I stood in silent vigil watching him and waiting to protect Mom if that should be needed. Pulling open the upper kitchen cabinet door, he reached up to the second shelf and pulled out his 45-caliber pistol and caressed it in his hand. His voice became quiet, nearly a whisper, as his demeanor changed and I felt my heart begin to race.

"Elva, I'm gonna do the same thing that Sam did."

"You mean that man you worked with?" Mom's voice quivered.

"Yea, he parked on the train track. A train hit him, and that was the end. I'll just put one through my head, and I'll be just like him, dead." He paused again for effect. Mom stood with her eyes fixated on the gun and held her hand over her mouth. I tried not to move. Maybe if I stood still he would forget I was there.

"You don't think I'll do it, do ya?" He glared at my mother. Mom froze, afraid of disagreeing with him.

"Virgil, I know you can do it, but I wish you wouldn't." She shook her head and I saw tears come to her eyes.

I swallowed hard, and broke my long-held silence, fearing the worst.

"Daddy, don't do it. We all love you," I cried out and reached my hand out to him. He didn't respond to my pleadings. My words pounded on a stone wall, and echoed back to me, unheard.

"Elva," he said to my mom. "Call my mother and tell her that I want to farm out there. Right now!" My mother and I both knew that this would do no good.

"If you don't call my mom and get her to give me some land, then I'll just pull this trigger," he said in a deep tone.

I couldn't take it anymore.

"Daddy, don't we count? We don't want you to die. Please don't do it."

"Your mother is not going to listen to me, Virgil, you know that," Mom pleaded.

"Well, you better hope she listens or I'm going to spread my brains all over this kitchen."

"Oh, Virgil, don't talk like that in front of Diana."

"I don't give a damn." I felt that to my core. I wished that I didn't care about him either, but I did.

"Alright—I'll call her." Mom heaved a deep sigh and dialed the phone.

There was a long pause as we all waited for the phone to ring and for Grandma to pick up on the other end.

"Hello, Alma, this is Elva. I'm sorry to bother, but things have gotten pretty bad here and Virgil is threatening to kill himself unless you give him some of the farm to work." She was quiet for a moment, shaking her head, listening to my grandma on the other end of the phone.

"I understand, but I'm not sure what he's going to do." Again, silence.

"I'll tell him," she said with her head bowed. There was a pregnant pause. "Your mom said no, Virgil."

Now, my mother and I waited without breathing.

"God damn her all to hell!" He slammed the gun back up on the shelf and stormed out the side door.

Behind, he left us standing stunned—like so many wounded soldiers on the battlefield. My mother went to her room, fell across her bed and began to cry. I followed and sat on the bed beside her and patted her back and told her how much I loved her. Her parents and her sister were no longer alive, and so she couldn't turn to them, now. I watched her as her strength gave way to despair, which my comforting did nothing to repair. When she finally went to sleep, I crept quietly to my room at the front of the house.

He didn't care that I loved him or that he had a wife and two other daughters who loved him, too. The pain that he felt, now was passed on to me—like some long held family treasure. I lay across my bed and rehearsed the scene over and over in my head. This incident would be repeated more than once, but never a hint of it would be shared with anyone.

CHAPTER FOUR

THE PICADOR

A picador is one of the pair of horseman in a Spanish bullfight that jabs the bull with a lance. Bullfighting is a blood sport, where the picador pierces the back of the bull's neck to straighten the bull's charge, fatigue the bull, and excite it to attack. The willingness of the bull to charge is often cited as the biggest test of its courage. By the time the bull was ready for the matador, his hide would be pierced many times and he would be weak from it.

My father was a picador. He enjoyed creating uproar. Perhaps it gave him some kind of release from his rage. My mother, of course, was his first target.

By the time I was a teenager of thirteen, I knew this. And I knew my role in the game. Dad pushed and pushed my mother's buttons until she would give into his jabs. My primary role had always been as an observer, and later as a comforter for Mom in the aftermath, but eventually I joined in the fight.

19

Mom walked in from work one cold fall night with a load of groceries for supper. I came into the kitchen and stood at the island, which held both the sink and a counter that served as a table, while she went about the business of cooking the meal. Soon pork chops sizzled in the frying pan, as boiling water splashed out from under the lid of a sauce pan.

My father was already home and pacing around the family room, which was an extension to the kitchen. He was muttering to himself, "Jim is just one of those Jew bastards. You think he's a great guy though, don't you?" Dad threw his voice toward Mom in the kitchen in an accusatory tone. Mom picked up a tomato and began to slice it, staring into the sink. Dad had a particular antipathy to Jewish people. Partly, at least, this was because he knew his racism would hook my mother.

I was used to this kind of thing. Verbal bullfights were a daily event. Mom would go about her business of being mother and housewife, after working outside the home all day. Once Dad started, she became like an animal that was pursued until it weakens and succumbs to the chase. She became trapped within the walls of the house. Dad would begin his onslaught of verbal lances meant to stir her into a confrontation.

"Jews are all alike. You can't trust any of them," he continued. "Hitler should have finished what he started." Mom did her best to ignore his comments and focus on her kitchen chores, but I knew he would keep thrusting spears in her direction.

"Well, I know your church believes the Jews are something special," Dad asserted. "Maybe your church is involved in the lies that the Jews always tell! They're behind all the wars, you know." I glanced at my father now, knowing he was treading on ground Mom couldn't ignore. Her church was important to her. Her father had been a pastor in the church while she was growing up. Mom's face began to flush and she moved more quickly with her knife and turned away from his steady stare. He was putting words in her mouth.

The picador had enraged the bull. Her pupils dilated, and her mouth got straight and tight. I could tell she felt the anger growing inside her, and I watched her make the decision to speak up.

Turning toward the family room to face him, she said, "Virgil, you know that the church has nothing to do with what Jews decide to do or not do, and neither do I."

"You think Jim is a great guy, don't you?" Dad insisted.

"You're the one who said that, not me," Mom replied as her voice became louder.

"Well, you believe you're in one of the tribes of Israel, right?" Dad replied pointing an accusing finger her way.

From my post in the kitchen, I felt my own inclination to engage in this blood sport rising. My longing was to protect and defend my mother. As usual, I stood on the edge observing the Picador and the bull. My heart was full of compassion for my mom—and fear on her behalf. She'd been working hard all day, and now she was being pummeled with verbal blows. I inhaled deep, and stood as tall as I could and jumped into the ring.

"Well, Dad, the Jews are from only one of the twelve tribes. They are from the tribe of Judah." Obviously, I had the mistaken belief at such a young age that you can bring sanity to insanity with reason. I felt, as adolescents often do, that I had some power to make a difference if I only put forth a good answer or offered a genuine solution.

"See, what did I tell you? That church of yours taught her that," he continued to glare at Mom while pointing in my direction.

"Not really. I read about it. It's in the old testament." Parry, thrust.

"You think I'm a heathen, don't you?" he asked. Pivot, thrust.

"I didn't call you a heathen," I said. The bull's head rose.

"All of your church members are hypocrites. Take Tom, your pastor. He thinks he's really good, but I've seen him walk by a hungry man and do nothing." Deep harpoon blow. As my father and I batted words back and forth, my mother turned her attention to the salad. She washed the lettuce, and the determination on her face dissipated as she stepped aside and let me take up the fight.

"All Christians are hypocrites," I said. "We all fall short of the glory of God, the Bible says."

I had said something that he couldn't, or wouldn't, respond to. I watched as his angry adrenaline began to evaporate. He had drawn another person into his game. With a quiet chuckle, he turned and slid out the door, and it was over. My mother and I didn't dare exchange glances. I was filled with sadness and confusion, and guilt for talking back to my father. I had been raised to respect my elders. With one heavy sigh, I turned from the kitchen and went to my room. In my room, I tried to collect myself, as I reviewed our conversation in my mind. What had caused him to call it quits?

What did he get out of it? He knew which buttons to push to get me involved, even as he knew how to hook Mom. Once I became accustomed to Dad's provocations, he would change his stance on the subject, to keep me off balance. It was always the same strategy no matter the subject.

My mother once told me that Dad was proud of me for being able to catch him and pin him down in an argument. In his mind, she told me, he was teaching me to be strong and make it in the world. I thought about another day, in another argument, when I'd said,

"Dad, you say that Jews are to blame for all the money problems in the world, but five minutes ago you said it was the gun and weapons manufacturers. Which is it?" Whenever I caught him in one of his switches, he smiled from ear to ear and laughed.

So that was it. He led us all on merry chases by switching his positions on subjects just to keep the uproar going. From one argument to another he would change what appeared to be his beliefs, because beliefs were not what was important. Like a good picador, his job was to keep the bull enraged. I had still lost.

And he was wrong that he was teaching me to be strong. How could he be so wrong? I didn't feel strong because I could argue or because I caught onto his tricks. I felt sad that this was the only way I could engage with him.

CHAPTER FIVE

BREAKING AWAY: I

Getting out of the house, away from the ever-present arguments, became an attractive alternative to participating in them. As time went by, I spent every opportunity with my church family. They were my refuge, but even that only lasted for an hour here and there. Even winning an argument was only a brief victory, and the battle would continue the next time Dad came into the house. I realized the time had come to break away from the constant barrage.

Money was always in short supply in my family. The idea of having my own wages free of any obligation to my parents enticed me. My parents neither encouraged or discouraged me. I was free to make many of life's decisions at this point and so I mentioned the job hunt in passing with very little acknowledgement.

My oldest sister, Cheryl, worked at the local A&W drive-in, and was spending her own money. I saw how independence looked, and I wanted it for myself. With her help to do my hair and makeup, I resembled an eighteen-year-old, instead of the fifteen-year old that I actually was.

I picked up an application from the front desk attendant for the Hotel Goodland. The front desk attendant was an older man with white hair who sat at the old wooden desk in the front lobby in his crumpled brown trousers and light green short-sleeved shirt. He taught art privately, and supplemented his art with this job. We knew each other in passing, because he had been teaching my younger sister for years. Mr. T. smiled and nodded recognition as I took the form. I took it home, and began answering the questions and later that day, I returned it to the front desk.

Three days later, after receiving a phone call from the hotel's manager. Cheryl dropped me off in front of the three-story hotel which took up over half a block on either side of the corner. I climbed the white cement steps up to the front door, and entered the heavy wooden and glass doors. I caught a whiff of old cigarette smoke and musty furniture as I walked across the black and white tile floor into the coffee shop. Sitting on a bar stool near the counter was a heavy-set man in black trousers, white shirt, black suspenders, and dark Oxford shoes.

"Hello, my name is Stewart. You must be Diane."

"Diana"

"Oh, yes."

"We need someone who we can rely on, who isn't afraid to work."

"I will do my best. What do you need me to do?"

"We have a maid who fell and broke her ribs. She has worked here for years, and will probably keep going until she can't go anymore. She is in her 70s and doesn't believe in Social Security. Veda will show you everything you need to know. You answer to her."

"Yes, sir."

"Okay, then, you start on Monday."

"Thank you very much sir. I will do my very best."

"Okay, okay." Stewart waved me off.

My stomach churned and I had this deep desire to run the other way on Monday morning. At no point in all the time I had been going to school had I ever felt this kind of fear. This was a whole new experience, and my sense of confidence was not as great as I had hoped. After taking some deep cleansing breaths, I got dressed and walked to the hotel. Veda was a short, petite, muscular 78-year-old Polish woman with fine white hair pulled up into a bun with small wisps that refused to comply. She wore a blue-grey cotton work dress with heavy support hose and black orthopedic shoes. Veda had done the job of cleaning the two upper floors of the hotel by herself for years. Veda showed me where things were kept and had me watch how she cleaned a room, and then I was on my own.

With some hesitation, I repeated what I had seen her do. Veda worked circles around me and was done with her floor before I had made it through half of mine. She just let out a loud sigh and shook her head when she came to see my progress. Her disappointment in me was palpable. It was hard to be out done by a woman sixty-three years my senior.

By week three at the hotel, I was doing better and the butterflies I had originally felt had passed. On two consecutive days that week, Veda and I were unable to get into one of the rooms on my floor to clean.

"Damn drunk, Edgar is. Every day a damn drunk," she said waving her finger at the locked door with vigor. Even at five feet tall, all the people that lived or worked there stepped aside for her. I didn't envy this man if she found him.

Day three arrived and finally Veda got the key to open Edgar's room. The odor of partially digested alcohol turned vomit nearly bowled me over. I gagged.

"Damn drunk! He puke and shit everywhere." Her face was red and purple with rage. "I go get mop. You start in bathroom."

I got the bleach, scouring powder, and cleaning rags from the cleaning closet up the hall. I began scrubbing and disinfecting. The room was dead quiet, but I had an uncomfortable feeling, and the hair on the back of my neck came to attention. I had never been around a drunk before, thank goodness. In the midst of my efforts I heard someone behind me.

Edgar stood in the doorway, and only exit from the bathroom. I turned to face him. The smell of old sweat and alcohol permeated the small-enclosed space. His dark brown hair was scruffy and dirty and had not met a comb for days. The beard on his face was several days old with dried vomit in it. His light blue work shirt had sweat stains and unknown food particles on it, and his dark wrinkled work pants were urine stained and torn at the knee.

Edgar's eyes were blood shot and glazed and his reaction time was slow, so that when he lunged for me, I was able to maneuver out of his grasp and out of the room with him not far behind. Veda met Edger in the hallway with mop in hand. The half-drunk man recognized her and knew he was in trouble, and began to retreat into his room as Veda advanced with the mop.

"You go home. I take care of this." Veda commanded. She didn't have to say it twice. I ran down the stairs and out of the front door of the hotel, and kept running for several blocks, before I finally slowed to a walk. Was this the best I could do? Was this the only kind of work I could get? I thought as I walked with my head bowed. Gradually, I heard a man calling to me from across the street.

"How's everything at the hospital?"

"The hospital?"

"Yea, how are things goin' up there?"

"Alright, I guess."

"Good to hear it." The man said as he returned to raking his yard.

Why had this man asked me about the hospital? I pondered for a moment, and then realized that I was wearing a white working uniform and white work shoes.

The man assumed I worked at the hospital since I had already run passed it on my way home. The idea that this man wanted my opinion and thought I worked at the hospital triggered in me a desire to make it be true. I discovered a deep need that I didn't even know was there. I wanted the kind of respect that I heard in that man's voice. Working as a hotel maid that cleans up after drunks would not give me that respect that I longed for. This need had to be filled. I called the hotel as soon as I got home and quit that job.

The next day, I climbed the large cement stairs up to the front of the old red brick hospital and opened the double white wooden doors and walked into the front lobby. The interesting combination of floor polish and antiseptic wafted up to my nose. The front desk was empty at that moment and across from it was a small waiting area with a half dozen chairs. The door to the second floor was open as it was visiting hours and just beyond it was the nursery. I remembered when my little sister was born and I first saw her there in her clear plastic bassinet. It had been a long time since I had been inside the building. I walked over to the large glass window and peered in at the newest members of the community.

Soon, I heard chatter at the desk as a visitor was asking questions about a patient. When the visitor and desk staff completed their business, I saw an opportunity to fulfill my purpose.

"Excuse me, my name is Diana Middleton, and I was wondering if I could get an application for employment?"

"Sure. What job are you applying for?"

"I'm not sure. What jobs are available when you are still in high school?"

"You could work in the dietary department, housekeeping, or as a nurse's aide."

"Do they have a different application for each one?"

"No. They will look over your answers and if you fit one of those jobs, they will contact you for an interview."

"Thank you so much. Can I fill it out over here and return it to you?"

"Sure, just leave it on the counter."

I went across from the desk and sat on a cold leather seat in the waiting area and carefully filled out the application before returning it to the front desk and thanking the woman who patiently waited there. I had to thank the hotel and Veda for giving me a sense of self-confidence that I hadn't had before then.

A week after I left my application at the front desk, I received a call from Mrs. K. She quizzed me about my grades and interests. She suggested that I consider being a nurse's aide. I took a deep breath and said yes. I wasn't sure what that job entailed, but it had to be better than being a maid at the Hotel Goodland.

Mrs. K.'s job was to train me and the other four students being prepared to work in the hospital. My only real experience with the hospital had been as a visitor and so I went into this arena as a fifteen-year-old novice. Every day after school for two hours we met in an empty patient room. We took turns being the patient as Mrs. K. taught us how to give a bed bath, how to change a bed with the patient in it, take vital physical information, how to place a bedpan or urinal, and how to transfer a patient from chair to commode. Without realizing it, I was also learning a new language: TPR, BP, UA, BM, and I and O. This training ended after two weeks and the real education began.

The hospital was divided into three floors. The basement held the emergency room, the delivery room for obstetrics, the surgical suite, and the kitchen. The second floor was surgical, maternity, and the nursery. The third floor was the medical floor. This was the floor where new nurse's aides began.

On my first night, I worked with Marge. She was over six feet tall and large boned with short blonde hair. For such an imposing figure, she had a quiet voice and meek demeanor. She was a professional from head to toe with a small dainty white nursing cap, white dress uniform, white hose, and shoes. She moved up and down the hall with barely a sound. Her primary purpose, beyond carrying out doctors' orders, was making sure patients were comfortable and pain free. This is where her guidance and reinforcement improved on the basics that Mrs. K. had given us.

At the end of one night, after the hall lights were dimmed and the night lights were lit, I began the final gathering of information from my assigned patients to give to Marge. As I passed the one three-bed ward on the floor, I saw Marge next to one of the beds and she motioned vigorously to me to come into the room.

"Diana, run downstairs and tell Vernice to call the doctor and tell him that this patient's heart has stopped and then get a cardiac needle and epinephrine."

I stood as though I was rooted to the floor, for a second, and then my brain went into gear as I ran down past the end of the bed and struck my leg on the "knee-knocker" bed crank. I limped as fast as I could to the stairs and went to the second floor. As I went, I repeated the directions Marge had given me over and over for fear I would forget, and prayed as I went. I saw Vernice, the RN for the surgical floor. Down the hallway she saw the look on my face and came directly to me. I repeated Marge's directions without missing a beat, and she flew into the nurse's station and came out with a long needle and a glass ampule and sent me back upstairs.

I ran back to the room where Marge waited and handed her the items and she proceeded to break the glass ampule and drew up the contents into the syringe. Soon after, Vernice joined Marge and then the doctor arrived. I stood at the doorway watching them work to revive this man. Marge stood over the man and pumped his chest, in between the doctor barking orders for Vernice. My heart was beating so loud I could hear it in my ears and my mouth felt like the Sahara. The man coughed and gasped in a breath. Both nurses quickly pumped up the blood pressure cuff as the doctor listened intently to his heart.

I began to tremble slightly and felt the fear that had finally caught up to me. Even so, it felt good that I could do what I had been asked to do. I had leapt from doing the chores of patient care to the edge of the greatest responsibility I had ever encountered. The reason for the respect shown to these health care providers was obvious. I didn't run away from this job as I had at the hotel, and instead I felt drawn to it.

CHAPTER SIX

BREAKING AWAY: II

I was assigned to work all three shifts at the hospital at one time or another; every weekend, holiday, and throughout the summers of my last two years in high school. Most of the other nurses' aides were high school students like me. My wages were tucked away for college, except for a very reasonably priced radio, and a typewriter. The evening shift worked best for me. The house would be dark and quiet when I got home and a confrontation with Dad was unlikely during those hours.

In the solitude of my room one night after work, I lay on my stomach across my bed with my hymnal and sang quietly, one hymn after another. I loved to sing. I had learned the love for such music from Aunt Marie, and from my mother, who could recall the lyrics to nearly every hymn in the book. With each hymn, the stress of the day drained away, and in its place was a sense of being loved by God. I understood then why Marie seemed so full of joy when she played them on the piano. That sense of God's love was healing and as I turned pages, I came across a hymn that I had never heard before. I read the lyrics. The song read like the most beautiful prayer.

"Spirit of God, descend upon my heart.

Wean it from earth through all its pulses move.

Stoop to my weakness, mighty as Thou Art,

And make me love Thee as I ought to love." Words by George Croly

As I read the verses to this particular hymn, I knew that I just had to learn the music that went along with them. I felt so moved that, though it was late, I crept out to the piano in the living room with a flashlight, and I began to play the melody with one hand.

I didn't hear Mom tiptoe from the back bedrooms into the living room.

"Diana, it's time you went to bed. We can hear you down the hall." Mom said in a whisper. She didn't want me to wake Dad up.

"Sorry, Mom. It helps me unwind to sing."

"I understand. Just do it more quietly, ok?" Mom smiled and turned to go back to her room.

"Mom, can I talk to you for a minute?"

"Sure"

"Do you remember when I went to that Billy Graham Crusade last year?"

"Yes."

"I had been taught in Sunday school and church and I knew all the stories, but suddenly that night, Jesus became real to me and I felt so full I was overflowing. I want to share his love, but I'm not sure how to go about it."

"What you do for those patients at the hospital is a good beginning."

"That's true."

"Sorry, honey, but I've got to get some sleep tonight, can we talk another time?"

"Sure, Mom, thanks. Love ya."

As she shuffled down the hallway, I thought of the stories Mom had told me about how she had left home at eighteen, by herself, from her hometown of 4,000 people in Iowa, to study weather in Kansas City. When she finished weather school, she was sent to the weather bureau in Goodland for six years before she met dad and married him. She had lived on her own and was self-sufficient.

When World War II ended, and the GIs came home, she had to give up her job to the veterans and never had another job as good as the one she'd sacrificed. The idea of her leaving home and making her way in the world struck me as the way for me to make a different life for myself.

In May of 1971, at the age of 17, I graduated from high school. My parents and sisters sat in the bleachers as one student after another was awarded scholarships. I received $1200 in work-study to go to Community College, which was 35 miles away. The scholarship included housing, tuition, and books for a year. Many times growing up, I had gone to camps and retreats, but I had never left home for good before. I knew that this would lead to permanent separation eventually.

The day before my first day of work at the college library, Dad drove me down the interstate to Colby. After driving in silence for most of the trip, Dad broke the spell.

"Sis, we're gonna miss you at the house."

"Yea, I know," I said half-heartedly. "This is a big leap."

"You'll be fine," he said

"I hope so."

The old green Plymouth station wagon pulled up the circle drive in front of the administration building and I climbed out the door. Dad climbed out of the car and helped me collect my suitcase and my bag of sheets, towels, and washrags. I gave Dad a peck on his cheek and began to lug my belongings up a long sidewalk to the dormitory. The double glass doors of the dorm squeaked as I pushed on them with my shoulder. A young woman looked up from behind a desk as I entered and asked me for my identification and information.

When the preliminary paperwork was out of the way, she showed me out a side door into a courtyard encircled by a one story high group of rooms. Upon opening the door to my assigned part of the dorm, I realized that there was a common living room and bathroom that joined four bedrooms together. Each bedroom had bunk beds, two desks, and two closets. I would get roommates sooner or later, but for now I was completely alone and sat at my desk and closed my eyes and let the moment pass slowly. This was the Y in the road and I had chosen a path.

Now, I was away from home. I would neither hear nor speak during the fights between the Picador and the bull. I'd always dreamed of a calm and loving home, but I knew I didn't have one. I was leaving the world I had known, and I would be pursuing an education so that I could walk away from any relationship if it turned into what I had grown up with. I was going to save myself.

CHAPTER SEVEN

THE COLLEGE OF HARD KNOCKS: I

I spent one year at Community College in 1971-72 and then transferred fall semester '72 to Fort Hays State University. Fort Hays had a couple of things going for it: a strong science program and a young man I was dating. Sam, my boyfriend, was built more like a boy than a man. He was five foot four inches tall, small boned, with short dark hair, neatly combed, glasses, and very little facial hair.

Sam was a member of my church and we had met first on some youth trips and church reunions. I was shy, but he kept trying to get my attention at the various gatherings. When I began to respond to his friendliness, he started to back off. I wanted so badly to have a boyfriend like my classmates had, so I set aside the fact that he was less than what I had dreamed of and pursued him, which was what Sam had in mind all along.

I'd started dating him during my senior year in high school and that continued throughout my freshman year at Colby. He had moved to Goodland to attend the Vocational-Technical school and study electronics. He asked me out, but most of our dates consisted of going to a drive-in restaurant and listening to music on his eight-track player. We necked in the car on most dates. Sometimes we talked, but Sam usually dominated the conversation.

Though he was not what I had envisioned as the love of my life, Sam was the only young man who had ever asked me out, and that was no small thing. I'd felt left out, as my peers had already been dating for quite a while. The fact that Sam continued to date me through-out my senior year in high school and on into my fresh-man year in college made him very important to my self-esteem and me to his.

When Sam left Goodland for a job near Hays, Kansas at the end of my first year at Colby, I was afraid that our fragile relationship would flounder and be lost. I made a rash decision to leave Colby, and the safety of work-study, to attend college at Hays. I untethered myself from my lifelines of friends and family. This required my finding a job to pay my college bills, rent, food, and transportation. Work-study at Colby was designed to work around my college schedule, but the job I looked for in Hays would decide how many courses I could take.

There was a job opening at a Mexican restaurant. It was on the main drag of town, and was often full of college students. The building was the ubiquitous stucco one-story with sombreros and piñatas.

"So, you have never worked in a restaurant before, I see." The owner said looking down at my application. He was middle-aged and was dressed more as a cook than the owner of a restaurant.

"No, but I'm willing to learn."

"Have you ever used a cash register?"

"Yes, I used one when I worked at the concession stand at a couple of football games."

"You should be able to handle it then."

The job entailed taking orders, serving large groups and keeping the orders straight, making the refried beans, washing dishes, and serving beer. I didn't drink and my mother had preached to me and my sisters about the sin of drink all the time we were growing up. She recalled a neighbor who self-destructed due to alcohol, and had herself grown up in a family of tea-totalers. Serving beer flew in the face of what I believed in, but it was all or nothing if I wanted this job. The end of my work day always coincided with the end of students' drinking and eating for the night, which was midnight. By the time I walked through the door at my apartment at the end of the day, studying seemed like almost more than I could muster.

Within the first three weeks of the fall semester at Hays, I drove to the house outside of Hays that Sam was renting along with one of his vocational school classmates. I drove up to the one-story white house and climbed the large cement steps and knocked on the door. My breath was making clouds as I stood in the dim porch light. Finally, Sam opened the door.

"Hi. What are you doing here?" he asked.

"I hadn't heard from you since the last time I was here, and I missed you."

"I wasn't expecting you to come over," Sam emphasized.

"Why? Is there a problem?" I asked.

"Well, after our last experience, I didn't think it was working out."

The last experience had included necking on the couch in the living room, and his best efforts to get me out of my top and bra. I had gotten up and run into the bathroom and locked the door, and broke down and cried.

"You mean because I wouldn't have sex with you the last time I was here?"

"Well, yes, I guess." He said moving his feet around and looking at the floor.

"I don't believe in having sex outside of marriage. I thought with you being a member of the church, you would already understand that."

"Yea, okay, but it's not working out."

"I want my things," I said suddenly.

"Your things?"

"Yes, I want my school picture and everything I've given you."

"You do?" he looked confused and stunned and stood motionless as if letting my request sink in.

"Yes, and I want them now," I said emphatically. I now understood what I meant to him. I was a conquest and those things represented his trophies. Within five minutes, he returned with a box with the requested items inside. He handed the box to me, and I turned to leave, suppressing my tears. I didn't want him to see me cry. I made a clean break with him, but part of me longed for him to try to stop me from leaving. He didn't.

I now felt the sting of separation from family, friends, and of course Sam. The environment that I lived in at Hays was much more isolating than anything at the college in Colby. At Colby, everyone knew my name and I could find one or two people to visit or make plans with. Goodland was a short drive from Colby if I wanted to see people I knew there. It was a three-hour drive to get to my parents' home from Hays, and I couldn't afford to go there every time I got lonesome. The class sizes at Hays, made me feel like a number instead of a person and the long hours of work made socializing nearly impossible.

The apartment that I shared with three other people was empty most of the time. Each roommate that I had was on their own schedule that didn't jive with mine. My oldest sister, Cheryl, had sensed that I was struggling. She sent me a card. When I opened the card, it had a cat hanging from a rope on the inside. It said, "Tie a knot and hang on." I must have looked at that card a million times just to convince myself that I could actually tie that knot.

The semester at state college was a difficult one. Twenty hours of college credit was a full class load which, along with 28 hours of work a week, just about did me in. The idea of taking fewer classes since I was working seemed like giving in to this mistake. Two weeks before finals were to be given I had reached the end of my endurance. With organic chemistry, zoology, western civilization, English literature, and of course the obligatory physical education credits, I bobbed just above drowning. Sleep didn't come easily, and when it did, I awoke early in the mornings for no reason. I had trouble eating and the constant heartburn made me think that I was developing an ulcer. Exhaustion crept into my bones. Finally, I gave in and called my parents to come and get me, and they drove me home, like a whipped pup.

At home, I was able to sleep and eat, and the distance from college had given me time to think. The circumstances at Hays had tested me in ways that I had never imagined. Now, I sank under the covers of my bed and did not come out all day, because sleep allowed me to separate myself from the sadness and hopelessness that had become an overwhelming part of every moment of everyday. When I finally did slip out of bed, I wandered around the house in my pajamas all day with my unkempt hair sticking out in every direction. After a few days, Mom had to remind me to take a bath and brush my teeth and get dressed.

After jumping up to sit on the counter in the kitchen, I watched my mom work on breakfast. I told her about how sad I felt while she cooked.

"Sis, you need to look around you and find everything you can that makes you feel good. Look at the blue sky or hear the birds singing," Dad said as if he'd experienced it himself.

"Okay."

"It helps to do that," he said as he walked out the door. Dad had never talked to me that way. He saw the depression that I had developed and recognized it. He was right. I changed my focus to the moment I was in now, instead of all the time that had already passed at Hays. It helped me to rally myself as I stiffened my spine. With a bath and clean clothes, I decided that I was not going to be defeated by this incident and so I asked Dad to drive me back to Hays to complete my final exams. My grade point average dropped that semester, but I finished what I had started. I couldn't help but wonder what my future would be after that semester was accomplished.

CHAPTER EIGHT

COLLEGE OF HARD KNOCKS: II

One Friday, after returning to Goodland to live, I joined Mom for her coffee break at the car dealership where she worked. We sat near the large front windows of the Cadillac/Pontiac dealership. A decrepit grey Chevrolet drove by and parked across the street. Greg, a friend from Colby, exited the car and walked toward us.

"Hey, I saw your car, and then there you were in the window, so I just thought I'd see what's happening with ya," Greg said as he walked in the front doors.

"Mom, this is Greg. We're friends from Colby." I wondered what Mom thought about Greg's black dress shirt, black jeans, boots, long straight black hair, and especially his black fingernail polish.

"Nice to meet you Greg," Mom said without fluttering an eyelash. Mom's partner in the parts department just shook his head silently when Greg walked close by. The auto mechanics from the attached shop were quiet, and one whispered to his peer and then they both chuckled, while looking towards Greg. I ignored the unspoken disapproval.

"Greg, I hit a snag at Hays, and so now I'm back living with my folks and working at the hospital again." I said in almost a whisper, feeling half-ashamed to admit my poor judgement.

Greg just shrugged his shoulders to indicate his indifference to what I felt was a major setback. He was not embraced by most of the people at Colby College. What other people thought of him never seemed to disturb him at all. He was eccentric. His front incisors were elongated, and he imagined sharpening them so he could look like a vampire. In spite of that, he was honest, pleasant, and accepting of others, so I overlooked his odd behavior, and enjoyed knowing him as a friend.

"Greg, it's sure good to see you. I've missed you and Colby."

"Well, why don't we just run over there and see what's up?"

"I haven't been to Colby for months. I wonder who'll be there? It's semester break, you know."

"Sure, but we can go to the administration building and visit the secretaries there," Greg said. "You know most of them."

"Yea, I haven't seen them for a long time. I don't have to work tonight. Sure, let's go. Is that alright, Mom?"

"Have a good time," Mom replied with the hint of smile on her face, as she got up and started walking back to work.

Greg and I ambled across the street, got into his car, and headed for the interstate. After a silent interlude, Greg asked, "What happened in Hays?"

The dry brown grass and skiffs of winter snow whizzed by outside the window as I avoided his gaze.

"Boy, did I screw up. I thought this guy Sam loved me. You remember me talking about him? I followed him to Hays, but he was only interested in one thing, if you know what I mean. I wasn't raised that way."

"Yea, I know the type," Greg replied.

"Now, I'm back to square one. I'm not sure what to do with my life, but I know I have to do something, because I don't want to wind up living with my folks forever."

"You'll think of something."

Soon we took the off ramp and then drove up the circular driveway in front of the administration building, past the library, the cafeteria and recreational center, and sidewalks empty of students. I felt a soft ache in my heart.

"Greg, this is so different than what I experienced at state college. There were so many students. I was a number. They didn't know who I was or care if I showed up for class. I was in such a big school, and I felt so isolated and alone. Colby is so much more friendly and warm and people know your name. I'm a small town girl."

"Yea, I know what you mean. I miss this place when I'm away."

The fact that I couldn't remove that mistaken semester and replace it with the more positive feelings that I had while at Colby left me feeling lost. Would the mistake I made by going to Hays this last semester end my prospects permanently? The break-up with Sam renewed my conviction that I needed to support myself and be independent. I wanted my choice to feel right, and be more carefully considered than my last major decisions. At 18, I saw myself as an adult, and responsible for my mistakes.

Greg and I pushed open the glass doors to the administration building at Colby Community College, and walked down shiny tile floors outside the offices, while I stuck my head in to say hello.

"Hey, Ruth, no rest for the weary," I chirped.

"That's for sure. What are you doing here?"

"Just missed the place and thought I'd come by and keep you guys honest."

"Well, somebody needs to," Greg chimed in and proceeded down the rows of offices sticking his head in each one.

I continued on down the hallway and stopped outside the student advisors' offices, and noticed a cork board with different school programs posted. Two of the programs listed were for nursing schools. I'd considered going into nursing but had dismissed the idea. I'd seen what RNs had to do when I worked beside them. Their job was a lot of responsibility. I thought the distance from the patients that the lab technologist had seemed more fitting for me, but organic chemistry was not my strong suit and it was necessary for the program.

One nursing program in Salina, Kansas required a class on nutrition, but the nursing program at a medical center in Wichita, Kansas, taught it during the program. The Wichita program did require human growth and development. I picked up a class catalogue and thumbed through it. I could take human growth and development during the summer. I leaned into the office of the secretary for the advisors and asked when the next nutrition classes would be given. There would be none until next year. I was lost in thought, feeling a terrible pressure to decide what to do before the next semester started.

"Hey, you ready to go?" Greg interrupted my reverie. I startled, gave one more glance at the flyers, and then nodded and followed him out to the parking lot.

On the way home, I batted the possibility of going into nursing back and forth with Greg. He told me that he knew I could do anything I wanted to do, but it seemed as though I was being drawn to nursing for some reason. He pulled in next to my car, and I bid him farewell. What to do? What to do?

CHAPTER NINE

CHARLOTTE

One spring Sunday in 1972, I was fortunate to have a day off from my work at the hospital. Dad, Mom, my ten-year-old sister Chris, and I rode to the farm in the brown Dodge. Cheryl now lived in the same apartment I had lived in at Hays and so we didn't see her as often. When we came to a halt on the gravel covered parking area in front of the main house, Chris exited the car and walked into the house and to the first table she could find, and started to draw, which was her favorite way to pass her time. I sauntered out to the windmill and turned the spigot with a squeak and water gurgled into an old tin cup that hung on a nail there. The water was better than any I had ever tasted anywhere else. I made my way back to the main house, and I entered through the front door, which led into the utility room.

Grandma's round face and pink cheeks greeted me at the door. She threw her arms around me with her well-known hug. She had grown grayer since the last time I'd been home.

"You look healthy," she said. "How was school?"

"It was hard but I finished the semester. I'll have to decide where to go from here."

"I bet you'll figure it out," she said with a final squeeze.

Many of my uncles and aunts, as well as my parents, were gathering in the dining room around the long cherry wood table. There was a large plate of fried chicken, and Aunt Marie placed an equally large bowl of potato salad next to it, and next to that was a lovely relish tray heaped with olives and radishes. Each family had brought food for a potluck to celebrate Easter. I hoped no one would ask me too many questions about what was next on the horizon for me because I didn't want to explain why I went to Hays and now was out of school. I hoped they would become occupied with other subjects.

"Diana, what are you up to now?" Aunt Marie asked without skipping a beat. This was just what I had been afraid of, a grilling about my future plans.

"I finished at Hays, and now I'm trying to figure out what should come next. I'm working at the hospital for now," I added, hoping that would bring the conversation to an end.

"Well, you seem to like that kind of work, don't you?"

"Yea. I'm used to it by now."

Grandma and I joined everyone else around the table. We bowed our heads and Grandma said the blessing. As everyone grabbed his or her eating utensils and plates, they started serving themselves. I stood at the end of the line that formed to go around the table.

"I remember when my grandma Charlotte used to take care of folks around these parts. I remember when she treated your grandpa for a big bruise on his leg," my dad mentioned. "She was smart about medical things."

"Yes, she used that strange instrument on him," Dad's brother replied. "It had two levers. She put it on his leg over the bruise and flipped one lever, which caused it to stick to his leg. Then she flipped the other lever, and blood shot clear up to the ceiling."

My oldest cousin rolled his eyes. 'That's gross," he said as he dished up some green beans and tossed a chicken leg on his plate.

"It had little blades in it," Grandma explained.

"How did your mom learn how to do that?" I asked my grandmother.

"Well, you know she was born in Sweden, and she lost her parents and was adopted by her uncle. Her uncle was a real doctor who took care of the King of Sweden. My mom followed him around and he taught her all these things."

Glad the focus was off of me now, I batted a question back at Grandma.

"So he actually taught her how to do more than nurses did in those days, right?"

"She became a midwife of sorts," Grandma responded.

By now we were all seated at small tables and chairs in the dining room. I sipped some coffee and took a forkful of macaroni salad.

"Do you remember when she vaccinated all of us kids for small pox?" Aunt Marie chimed in.

"Yea," my dad said. "She made the vaccine from cow pox," he added shaking his head with pride at his grandmother Charlotte's ingenuity.

"That's how they made the original small pox vaccine," I interjected. I'd learned this in my biology class last year.

"Back then there weren't many doctors out this way." Grandma said, "Doc Gulick hadn't arrived yet—she was the only one who could help people around here. She delivered babies, pulled teeth, set bones. She even helped me take care of Grandpa Middleton, your great grandpa, when his lungs filled up with fluid."

"She saved my life when I thought I would choke to death from diphtheria. I remember her walking through the house with some sulfur, which she was burning. It smelled like rotten eggs. She made your grandma close all the windows tight and pack any cracks with rags," Aunt Marie shared. The family obviously took pride in her abilities. It was as though she was reaching down through the years to grab my attention.

After dinner, I helped with the dishes and then told Grandma Middleton that I wanted to walk in the yard. I ambled down the same hill I used to rush down when I was a child. I came to the outstretched arms of the old mulberry tree that looked out over the wheat fields. I sat myself down on the moist grass under the tree and leaned back against its rough bark. The green shafts of

wheat were starting to get tall. They moved rhythmical-
ly with the breeze in a hypnotic way, which allowed me
to focus on my situation. First there were the flyers in
the college lobby and now this revelation that my great-
grandma Charlotte had basically been a doctor. I closed
my eyes and asked God, "Are you trying to tell me something?" A quiet knowing rose up inside me.

"Yes."

Back inside the house, Mom sat at the kitchen table
sipping coffee.

"Mom, I need to run some ideas by you, if that's alright."

"Sure," she said motioning to a chair. I sat myself
across from her.

"When I went to Colby last week, I saw information
about nursing schools. I don't think that I'm cut out
to be a laboratory technician like I thought I would be
when I left for Hays. What do you think about nursing
as a career?"

"Remember what I told you a long time ago about
how you could serve God? People are at their most vul-
nerable when they're sick. I know you would never leave
a patient that needed your help. You could be there for
them," she replied.

I sat staring into a cup of coffee and got to thinking
about great-grandma Charlotte. The thought occurred
to me that I wanted to be like her.

"I can get into a nursing school in Wichita by this
fall."

"That sounds like a good idea then," Mom said with a smile and a pat on my arm.

As our conversation died down, I noticed Grandma listening from the dining room. She disappeared down the hallway and turned left into her room. Mom and I returned to the dining room where the others were starting on dessert. Grandma Middleton walked across the dining room and into the kitchen and motioned for me.

"Diana, I've got something for you," she whispered and led me into the kitchen, "I want to help you. Don't tell anyone about this. Your cousin asked me for money to pay for college, and I turned him down." Grandma Middleton handed me a check for $1200. I was flabbergasted. I had worked in the college library through my first year at Colby Community College and at the taco restaurant in Hays because my parents didn't have the resources to pay my way through school. Dad did what he could by taking the engine from a used 62 Bellaire that I had bought and rebuilding it so that it ran like a top. It allowed me to travel to and from school, but I had to handle my own tuition, books, and housing, and financing the rest of my education was something I had not figured out yet.

"Grandma, this money will change things for me. I wasn't sure how I was going to afford to go on in school."

"Nursing school," she smiled.

"Yes, nursing school," I replied and gave her a big hug. I felt sad for my cousin, and hated keeping secrets from the rest of the family. I was becoming aware of more and more secrets that the family protected, but not the reason for such secrecy.

I wandered out of the kitchen through the utility room, and back out the front door. The air was warm and laden with the smell of fresh grass and the irises were beginning to bloom along the sidewalk. This had been an eventful evening, and I felt the gravity of the decision that I was making. For all my father's faults, he was also the kind of man who would be the first to come to the aide of someone who was injured or hurt. I imagine that Charlotte had influenced him in that direction while he was growing up.

I'd always been impressed with Dad's willingness to jump in and help. He had been a volunteer fireman for years. One day when I was a senior in high school, he had come home from reading meters and told me about an event that had happened that day. He had been down reading the meter near the side of one of the town's big restaurants when he heard this loud crack come from somewhere above him. He heard a man yelling for help and he climbed onto the roof to see what was going on. One workman was jumping up and down and pointing to a fellow lying on the roof with smoke coming off his neck where he had backed into an electric wire. The poor guy was still breathing, but not well. Dad used the wooden handle of a shovel and shoved the worker off the wire, and then pulled him away. Dad gave him rescue breaths to get him going again, and kept him alive until the ambulance got there. I remembered a nurse, Marge, doing that on a patient at the hospital.

With a history like mine, it seemed destiny that I would join my great-grandmother Charlotte in caring for the sick and injured. For once my father and my grandmother agreed on something: they were both proud of my choice, and I imagined that Charlotte would have been also. Charlotte had reached down through the years, and touched my imagination.

CHAPTER TEN

WESLEY SCHOOL OF NURSING

Sprawling over many blocks at the north end of Hillside Avenue in Wichita, Kansas, was Wesley Medical Center. Attached like an appendage to this trauma center of eight-hundred bed capacity was the Wesley School of Nursing and the dormitory that housed the twenty-something year old student nurses. Wesley was the nursing school that I had chosen, and the money Grandma had given me got me started well. There were government loans that made up the difference. The nursing dormitory made it easy to have housing while attending school.

Stacked three stories high, the nursing dormitory housed most of the students in the school. Second floor students were those I knew best. Each room on that floor housed two young women, along with their desks and books. Bent over those desks and books were young women tasked with learning nursing theory.

I had become roommates with a young woman named Mary. She was very studious and had a real talent for organizing patient care on the patient floors. She was slightly taller than me and had long thick brunette hair with a slight wave which she kept neatly wrapped in a variety of scarves. She was a very staunch Catholic, and I was a very staunch member of the Reorganized Church of Jesus Christ of Latter-Day Saints. We realized that neither of us would change our denomination, and so instead of arguing religion, we had shown each other respect for our beliefs and answered questions about them. Our questions about religion answered for the day, we would turn the light out for the night, and rehearse our day for one another, which often led to humorous banter. Because Mary was so accepting of me, and me of her, we became close friends. I felt more comfortable in the dorm than I had felt anywhere for many years.

Many times, while Mary worked on her studies in our room, I would sit on the black leather couch across from the television in the carpeted portion of the common room. For some reason I could concentrate better with the background noise. Only one other person joined me there late at night—Sophia. She sat at one end of the couch, in her boots, jeans, doe-colored leather coat with fringes, and her long blonde hair. Slender and slightly taller than me, we both had a tomboy feel.

Eventually, studying turned to chatting. Enjoying John Denver lyrics was something we had in common. Talking into the night, we discussed them, as well as sharing "The Prophet' by Khalil Gibran. A serious person most of the time, her humor was much more entertaining because she could do it with a straight face. This camaraderie continued on for several weeks.

Late one Friday night, we decided to walk down the short hall, through the school of nursing, and to the hospital. Walking past the beauty shop in the hospital proper, we made our way to the coffee shop, got drinks and snacks and started to return to the dorm.

"Hey, there's a good-looking guy coming our way. What do you think?" I whispered to Sophia.

"I'd give him an eight. He has a nice beat and he's easy to dance to." She replied with a wink. I laughed out loud at the American Band Stand reference, and then slapped my hand over my mouth and giggled under my breath all the way back home.

After that night, I saw Sophia less and less and then only in passing. We would smile at one another and say hi. She had told me that her parents had stopped paying her way through school because they didn't approve of how she lived her life. I didn't really know what about her life they disapproved of, and she never told me. Because of that shortfall in finances, she began to spend all of her spare time working as a nurse's aide, which left no extra time to study in the common room. I couldn't imagine being able to keep up with all that was required of us without having that spare time to unwind.

By October of my senior year, I was into my psychiatric rotation. Before we got to the psychiatric ward, our instructors explained the symptomatology we might encounter with various diagnoses and as they did, of course, people I knew came to mind. They warned us not to try to diagnose ourselves or those we knew. My aunt Marie, for example, had some paranoid concerns about people overhearing her conversations and had even once called my dad to have him come out to her house because she swore she heard people talking about her outside her home. He'd gone out there, walked around the house, and reassured Marie that no one was there. Even I had experienced depression after my boyfriend broke up with me while I was at school at Hays. I had to stop and laugh at myself for falling into the trap that the instructors said was pretty common in this field of study.

One Tuesday morning in my rotation, I was assigned to shadow a short, stocky black woman who was diagnosed as a paranoid schizophrenic. The woman had her hair carefully styled and bronzed with hair spray. The makeup around her eyes was extensive and her lipstick was a bright shade of red. Someone told me that she took up to three hours to accomplish this look.

As I walked into the lobby of the unrestricted unit, she was sitting at a table by the elevators with her back to the wall, which was her way of keeping people from being behind her. I approached her to say hello and she jumped up, came as close to my face as she could get without touching me, and started talking fast. I backed away out of her zone. My heart leapt into my throat. I wasn't sure what to do. "Annie," I said, "can you sit back down?" But Annie didn't want to. One of the unit nurses passed us and Annie ran up to her and repeated her nose-to-nose diatribe. I took that moment to calm myself down. Annie had discovered how to use the personal space of others to establish personal space for herself by making them back away from her. I learned right there that being mentally ill did not mean being stupid. I would have to be sure to earn her trust and give her space.

One day, I was in Annie's room as she went through her extensive rituals to get prepared for the day. She stood at the sink in her room and in front of her was a mirror where she applied more makeup and hair spray. I stood back out of what seemed to be her comfort zone. She looked in the mirror, made sure she could see me in it, and then began to sing.

"The water and the blood, from his wounded side did flow." This was as close to direct communication with me that she had made. The nurse in charge of her care entered the room, and Annie immediately stopped singing.

"Annie needs to go to the first floor and down the long hall to a diabetic class. You will need to go with her," the unit nurse instructed me.

"Alright. I think she's about done here," I replied.

"Good. Take her down, and then come right back up here."

Once on the elevator on the fifth floor, I pushed the button for the first floor. It was just Annie and I in the elevator. As soon as the doors closed and the elevator started its descent, Annie began singing again.

"The water and the blood..."

The elevator stopped on the fourth floor and the doors opened and two other people got on. I had an uncomfortable feeling that Annie might burst into song when the doors closed, but she stood stone faced and quiet. At the second floor, the doors opened again, the two people who had previously gotten on exited and, as soon as the door closed, Annie's song began again. She sang in almost a whisper for the next two floors, and then after we disembarked, she continued all the way down the hall, being sure to stay close to me. We entered the classroom at the end of the hall, where I was supposed to leave her. She took two steps into the room, and immediately backed out and began back up the hallway to the elevators. I followed closely behind her, and again she sang to me as we went up the hallway and back into the elevator to the 5th floor. The music was meant for me. I had gained a level of her trust.

The next day, her talking became much louder and more forceful and she became agitated, animated, and more confrontational. Her hair was in disarray and her eyes were wide and darting about. I stood on the sidelines with my eyes fixed on the nursing staff who surrounded her and made her walk to the locked unit, which was straight down from her usual location by the elevators. As she was escorted through the glass doors of the locked unit, I heard the doors click shut. Later, that day, I discovered that I would be shadowing her in the locked unit. When I arrived on the closed unit the next week I learned that her diagnosis had been changed to manic-depression (bipolar disorder), and she had been started on a new drug called lithium.

"Hello, I'm Diana Middleton and I am the student nurse who is supposed to follow Annie." I said into the intercom outside the locked unit door five days after Annie's admission to this unit. A buzzing sound came in response to my inquiry and I was able to open the heavy glass doors to the unit. I fully expected to see Annie in full regalia pushing people out of her personal space as she had done since I first met her two weeks ago. This was a very small unit compared to the open unit, but I didn't see her anywhere.

"Is Annie still a patient in this unit?" I inquired.

"Yes, she's over there on the sofa," the charge nurse replied.

There, sitting on the sofa, was Annie with her hair in curlers, wearing a robe over a patient gown, and slippers. She had propped her feet up on the coffee table in front of her.

This was a dramatic change in behavior. She sat with other patients within a few inches of her, and seemed perfectly comfortable.

Her manic behavior was greatly reduced within a week of the start of treatment. Lithium had only been used in the United States for manic-depression (bipolar disorder) for three years at that point. For the first time since I had known her she was still and serene.

Annie had been in state hospitals for over 30 years, starting when she was seventeen. Her diagnosis had been paranoid-schizophrenia for all that time. She had been getting in people's faces for most of her life, and now she sat quiet and calm. I would never forget this medication or the look of that manic woman when the staff had to surround her and drag her to the locked unit.

Toward the middle of November of my senior year, all the students were sweating out their case studies, and I was fully into mine on psychiatric nursing. Annie had been admitted as a paranoid schizophrenic and received a change in diagnoses. That meant that I had to write all there was to know about both diagnoses and explain why the change was made, and the result of the change. This made for a much more extensive paper.

It was Saturday night on the last weekend for us to finish them. I took a short break to watch TV. Several students with the same idea were gathered in the common room. While we were watching a mindless program, Sophia, dressed in a t-shirt and shorts, came in and lay down on her stomach on the floor in front of all of us. Pulling her hair over her face, she reached out toward us with one hand and then the other. Several of us made eye contact with one another, wondering what her strange behavior could mean.

"Sophia, are you fooling around?' I inquired. The rest of my classmates shrugged their shoulders or ignored her behavior. It was not unusual for people on the second floor to kid around. She didn't reply. Instead she just continued reaching out to us periodically. When the evening ended and it was time to go to bed, her behavior was soon forgotten.

Sunday morning was the time to leave the dorm, some for church, others for shopping or a movie. The dormitory emptied out. By late afternoon of this particular Sunday, I was back at the grindstone at the desk in my room, typing madly, as was Mary. My head was full of psychiatric theory as I made my first run for my coffee pot, which was kept in the kitchenette. As I began to return to my room, another friend, Toni, approached me. Hers was the first room across from the kitchen, and it just happened that I was there at that particular time.

"Diana, could you take a look at Sophia? I thought she was asleep, but I'm not so sure now," she explained with a look of apprehension on her face. Toni was usually happy-go-lucky, with a little orneriness thrown in, but that had evaporated.

"Sure, Toni, I'll look at her for you," I said quizzically. Toni walked into her room and sat on her bed across from Sophia's bed. Walking in, I noticed that Sophia was still and stiff in appearance, and her color was pale purple and yellow and rather wax-like. Her eyes were opened slightly, but not seeing. As I reached her bed, I could see dried mucous beneath her nose. Touching her arm, I noticed that it was cold and rigid. There was no rising and lowering of her chest and I could neither hear nor feel air movement from just above her face.

"Toni, Sophia is dead," I said. Frozen where she was sitting, Toni stared at Sophia's body. I walked to the telephone, which was on the wall near the room door, and dialed the front desk.

"Wesley School of Nursing," the operator nearly sang into the phone.

"Mrs. Welty, I need Mrs. Krumsick to come to room 201, right now."

"What do you need her for? She's in her apartment right now."

"Please send her up here now, Mrs. Welty. It's important, and I'll explain it to her when she arrives," I pleaded.

Mrs. Krumsick was near retirement age, was responsible for every student in the dormitory, and had a reputation of overreacting. I was concerned about her reaction if I had told her over the phone of Sophia's death. I thought it best to tell her in person. Shortly, she was at the doorway to 201.

"Sophia is dead, Mrs. Krumsick," I reported. Shock suddenly took the place of my sense of duty, as I walked by her to the couch in the next room. I sat down and stared at the TV. In a short time in the background, I heard the commotion, as the code team came running up the short hall with a patient cart and their equipment. I heard shouting, but I was in another place in my mind.

The sun set hours later and I was still sitting there. Numbness had enveloped me, and people's conversations rushed by me like car lights on the highway. Walking slowly down the long hall to my room, there was a feeling of extreme emotional exhaustion. Lying down on my bed, I closed my eyes but all I saw was Sophia all over again. Arising from the bed, I made my way downstairs to the first floor common area, which was many times larger than the one on second floor. Entering the room was like walking into a beehive. People were holding each other and many were crying. A young man from the class behind me kept saying,

"It's all my fault. Why did she do it?"

Another person said, "Was there a note?"

Until then, I had not even thought about a note. I saw none.

"There wasn't a note," I said. But no one acknowledged me because of the hubbub.

Suicide leaves nothing but questions. Most of those bring guilt to the survivors, especially if you're studying to be a nurse. Why didn't we pursue what Sophia was doing on the floor the night before she died? Perhaps it was because antics took place in that room all the time. Why didn't she tell me that she was having so much trouble? I knew she was having trouble, but I had no idea that it was out of control. Did I even know what all the problems were? How can you know what is going on in someone else's mind? Thoughts continued to spin and spin.

"God, why did you let this happen?" I yelled at him in my mind.

In return, I heard in my consciousness the scripture, "All things work for good to those who love the Lord."

I thought, "How can this possibly work for good! Sophia is dead and I could see no good that could possibly come from that."

Finally, warm salty tears quietly streamed down my face.

On Monday, school was shut down. An assembly was held in the large basement classroom where particulars concerning Sophia's funeral were announced, including that it would be held, in the church where her father was pastor, on the coming Thursday. We were informed that Sophia had overdosed on pills. Dean of the school, Mrs. D., opened the meeting to questions. The biggest question of course, was why. Most students wondered if something they had done or not done was the cause. She refused to disclose any information or anything about a suicide note. Wondering was all we could do. Later, after the meeting, I was told, by those who knew another facet of her life, that her sister had been killed in a car accident several years ago. Her parents were now bereft of children and future grandchildren. Why had she kept her life such a secret?

By Tuesday night, after not sleeping since Saturday night, my friend Nancy asked me how I was, and I told her that I kept seeing Sophia over and over. Nancy was helping where she could. She had taken in Toni as her roommate.

"Lie down, Diana, I'll lay next to you," she suggested. She was as good as her word, and finally I was able to sleep and escape for a while.

Wednesday morning, I called my oldest sister, Cheryl, because she was closer to Wichita then the rest of my family, and I begged her to come see me and explained why.

By the late afternoon, Cheryl met me at a restaurant and we went to a secluded corner. I had no appetite but had a deep desire to talk. Shortly after I told her that I had found a student nurse that I knew, dead in her room, she interrupted me and began to tell me about the trouble that she was having with her husband and stepson. This was an on-going saga in her life. Listening was all I could do. There was no relief here.

Thursday arrived and the entire school prepared to go to the funeral. The teachers were all there and the entire staff made sure that every student had somewhere to go for Thanksgiving, which would be coming up. As we filed into the church, volunteers seated us in the pews. I felt as though I might explode. It was hard to breath and I felt the pressure of tears that would not come, a type of numb pain. Particulars of the funeral made no impact on me, since my mind refused to take them in. As the funeral concluded, the time had come to walk up front by the casket and file out the door. Volunteers came up the aisle, and one stopped at my pew. I would be the first to file past the open casket. There was Sophia lying with makeup on to try and hide the ugliness of death that I had already seen. I kept telling myself to just keep walking. My walk was about to turn into a run when I found myself outside. One of my favorite teachers, Mrs. Rogers, came up to me.

"That was so unfair. When I saw them walk up to you, I thought 'Oh no, not her.' I am so sorry." She hugged me and held me as I was finally able to let go of my tears and sob into her shoulder.

All her students loved Mrs. Rogers. She was well known for her large infectious smile. When I had taken rehabilitative nursing from her, I remembered being at a retirement home that she had helped develop. One woman who lived there had a massive stroke that left her unable to speak. When she saw Mrs. Rogers coming, her face would light up and she would make a motion above her head with her thumb and forefinger open and then pull them together as if trying to visually make a point in the air, because Mrs. Rogers' nursing cap came to a point. They would embrace one another like the friends they had become.

She had both the training and the talent to reach people of all generations and bring them together. Not only was she a nursing instructor, but also a funeral director, who worked with her husband, a mortician. Teaching death and dying was in her wheel-house. Listening, really listening, is a sought-after gift, which she had in spades. For that reason, when she invited me to come to her home after the funeral, I didn't need to think long.

The rest of that day was spent in her home with a few other students. She put us at ease and fed us. In a very subtle way, she led us into a conversation about Sophia and what her suicide had felt like for each of us. Others spoke about the questions in their minds and about their responses to Sophia in the past. This relieved my mind about not being the only one. The next day, I sent her a thank-you note.

The case study that had been interrupted by these events was finished and handed in. I spent the last week required for psychiatric nursing. Upon returning to the dorm at the end of that day, I found a note from Mrs. Rogers which read:

Diana—I've read your letter over many times, and I guess I just haven't had an opportunity to tell you how very much it meant to me—it did. How very thoughtful of you. I know I for one have passed by telling people I appreciated them when I honestly felt it, but just didn't tell them. The richness of my knowing you and others here at school is great. I treasure that. Take care, Diana—welcome back to school—have a good semester—enjoy the challenge. —Frances Rogers

Her invitation to look forward instead of back served as the stimulus for me to continue in my studies. Time passed, and a group was formed with the hospital chaplain to help students deal with difficult times. I volunteered to work with him and several others. This was my penance for Sophia.

CHAPTER ELEVEN

GETTING TO KNOW YOU

Life at the dormitory at Wesley was only a portion of my life. The people at the dormitory were unfamiliar to me when I first arrived. I was a stranger in a strange land, looking for something I recognized. I walked in the front doors of Central Congregation on a warm fall day in 1973, shortly after arriving in Wichita for nursing school. I had a sense of anticipation. Central congregation in Wichita was much larger than my home congregation, but it didn't feel strange because I knew I shared common beliefs with the people inside.

I passed through the front glass doors and up a staircase toward the sanctuary. Dressed very business-like in a red suit coat and skirt, with her black hair coiffured to a tee and an amiable smile on her face was Dorothy Dodds, who introduced herself, shook my hand, and gave me a printed order of service. Dorothy did this every Sunday that she could. Her religion was dear to her heart.

After the service, members of the congregation took turns either hugging me or shaking my hand. Along with my hug from Dorothy was an invitation to lunch. She and I walked a few blocks to her house. The white and brown house was small but well kept, with a small yard, shrubbery along the front, and a small cement porch. As we entered the front door, a gentleman walked through the small kitchen opposite us and exited out the back door. Settling myself in a chair in the living room, I waited for lunch.

"Diana, we're ready to eat, if you would like to join us."

"Thank you Dorothy."

"Diana, this is my son, Mark." Dorothy said pointing to a slender young man seated at the table. The dining table was fitted in between the kitchen counter and the wall in a very tight squeeze.

"Nice to meet you, Diana," Mark said, motioning to an empty chair. Mark stared down at his plate and rarely changed his gaze, as I was seated next to him.

"What brought you to Wichita, Diana?" Dorothy queried.

"I'm going to nursing school at Wesley."

"What made you decide to go there?"

"They teach their nutrition throughout their coursework, so I was able to start nursing school sooner than other schools in the state."

"Well, we're glad that you came," she said with a smile as she passed the potatoes.

"Thank you, Dorothy. It's nice to get to know people in the church here in Wichita. It's a lot different here than in my home town."

"Where is your home town? Dorothy probed.

"I'm from Goodland, Kansas. It's up in the northwest corner of the state. There are about 5 thousand people living there."

"I've heard of it," Dorothy said with a nod.

"Yes, it's either the hottest or coldest place in the state."

"It seems that way," she said as she cut her roast.

"Can I ask who the gentleman was who left out the back door when we came in?"

"That's Jack. He's my husband. He runs a furniture store and he had to go to work. I work in real estate," she explained, pausing to pass the green beans. "He cooks a roast every Sunday, while we're at church."

"He does a really good job with it. The roast is delicious."

Mark remained quiet throughout the meal, but I was convinced he was listening to the back-and-forth conversation. When the meal was over, I helped Dorothy and Mark clear the table.

"Thank you, Dorothy. It was so kind of you to invite me into your home. Mark, it was nice to meet you. Thank you for a lovely meal. I'm sorry but I've got to get back to the dormitory and work on some homework."

"You're welcome, Diana. I hope to see you again next Sunday."

"I'll be there. Have a good rest of your day." I said as I waved good-bye and exited out the front door. The trees were every shade of red, yellow, and brown, and leaves silently drifted towards the ground and crunched as I walked over them and climbed into my car to drive back to the dorm.

As time passed that year, I became involved with the other adults my age at church. There were camping retreats, holiday activities at different homes, and eventually hosting worship services in various congregations around the area. Being a young single woman, I was of course aware of young men. One young man that I dated from this group turned out to be what my sister used to call an octopus—his arms were everywhere. There was not a second date with him. I later became enthralled with the leader of the group, Tim. In spite of my best efforts to gain his attention, I found that I was one among many young women hoping to catch his eye. He didn't see me as I hoped he would.

Talking to my mom about my longing for Tim and the lack of reciprocation, she suggested that I cast my eyes around and see if there was someone who was trying to get my attention. She suggested that I was being blinded from others who might want to socialize with me. Knowing my mother to be wise, I set aside my feelings about Tim and kept my eyes open.

From time to time, I would meet Mark after church and he would speak a few halting words to me. He stuttered but it didn't really ruffle me. Waiting for him seemed only polite and I found it was easier for him to complete his thoughts. Being aware that I was a student nurse, he would often tell me about his experiences as an orderly and at times, it seemed as though he was trying to impress me with how smart he was. He was knowledgeable about hospital care, but first impressions can be wrong, so I decided to get to know him better

After the first of the year, I received a phone call in my dorm room.

"Miss Middleton, this is Mark Dodds, would you wa-want to attend a con-concert with me?

"Sure. When will it be?"

"Wo-would tomorrow e-evening at six be alright?"

"You will need to pick me up at the front desk of the dorm. Do you know where it is?"

"Yes, I-I'll be there. Good night."

Knowing this young man to be so shy and having to overcome that as well as his stuttering made me feel special. He had to work up a lot of courage I was sure.

At the front desk of the dorm the next evening, I signed out and he walked me to his light blue 68 Pontiac, and opened my door for me. He appeared to be a gentleman. A line of demarcation was evident with him on one side of the car and me on the other side by the door, being careful not to touch. Shyness went both ways.

Arriving at a local restaurant, he continued to be the gentleman opening doors and assisting me with my chair. I was ashamed to think that this was the first date that I had been on that didn't include fast food. While awaiting our repast, I noticed his fine brown hair, which was neatly combed. His eyes were blue-green and he wore wire-rimmed glasses. At 5 foot and 8 inches in height, he was taller than me, and was dressed in a dark blue suit. No other date had ever dressed so nicely to take me out.

After our meal, we drove to downtown Wichita, where we parked near Century 2, a large convention center. He escorted me to my seat as we prepared to listen to Ferrante and Teicher of piano fame. A concert was another first for me. This date was head and shoulders above any other I had ever had.

On our way out of the concert, the sky was full of stars and it was very cold. My coat pockets were full of this and that, and so I put one hand in his coat pocket. Mark was startled at first, but shortly seemed to like the company of my hand next to his. He opened the car door for me and then walked to the driver's side door, and he slid behind the wheel.

Arriving at the dorm, he walked with me from the parking lot and up the sidewalk until it turned towards the dormitory door. Holding my hands in his, he said,

"Thank you for a lovely evening."

Before I could reply, he bounced away like a frightened deer. I smiled to myself. His sweet shyness was endearing.

For the next several months I would visit after church much as I had done before. Chipping away at his formal wall, I talked to him about his graduating from

Friends University the summer before I arrived, with a bachelor's degree in science. Mark shared information on his family off and on. The tete-a-tetes that Mark and I had usually lasted less than five minutes at a time, yet we were getting to know one another. He told me that his mother had been married before she married his dad, but her first husband had died of cancer. Susan was his half-sister by that marriage. His father, Jack, had known Dorothy since they were teenagers when they had both joined the church. Jack had been engaged before he married Dorothy, but his fiancée's parents had not approved of him, and therefore she did not follow through with the marriage. Jack had never forgotten being passed over and unfortunately the people involved had been church members. Even after nearly 25 years, every Sunday was a trial for Mark and his mother as Jack resented their continuing to go to that church. Pausing at the end of the block before turning towards the house of worship, Mark had to choose between it and his dad.

I went home to Goodland for the summer of '74 and worked as a nurse's aide. Work kept me busy all summer and I didn't communicate with Mark, or he with me. As fall approached, I prepared for my second year in nursing school.

Fall passed as I dug into my studies and then Sophia's suicide happened. When 1975 dawned, I needed to refill my cup. The choir director at church, who was also a high school music teacher, decided that we would do an Easter choral production. The music was wonderful and

I loved to sing. Suddenly, Mark developed an interest in music as well. I suspected that his new interest had to do with me. We practiced every Sunday afternoon and Wednesday evening after prayer service. I was coming to care about Mark more and more with each talk that we had. One evening after Mark and I had climbed the stairs to the choir loft, I paused, stood on my tiptoes, kissed him on the cheek, and skipped on to choir. To say Mark was struck dumb was not an exaggeration.

I wasn't sure whether the kiss would motivate him or frighten him away, but I knew that I had waited long enough for a second date. Soon after my amorous advance, Mark invited me to the Valentine's Day party, which would be at the church in two weeks. I agreed immediately to his request, and then I was called almost daily "to confirm" our date. His insecurity didn't bother me, and his sigh of relief each time I "confirmed" our date again was charming.

As February began, Mark took me to his house for a snack before we were to go to choir. The phone rang and the rule of the house was not to let it ring more than once because of Dorothy's real estate business. Standing between the phone and the Dodds family could be harmful to your health.

"Well, who's on the phone?" Jack demanded as he came in the back door leading to the kitchen.

"It's-it's Laura fr-from chu-church."

"Speak up, I can't understand you."

"It's L-Laura."

"Well just hang it up!"

Watching this scene made me want to jump up and tell Jack to back off, but I bit my tongue.

Attired in a short-sleeve white dress shirt and dark business slacks, Jack was shorter and heavier than Mark, with black slicked down hair, large ears, and jowls for cheeks. He was stocky from his hips on up to his shoulders with thin legs from the waist down, and appeared to have insufficient butt to hold up his pants. He ignored me, which I took as a kindness. Dorothy never said a word to Jack about his badgering of Mark, or that Mark's stuttering seemed to worsen when he was around. Even Susan, Mark's married half-sister, didn't stand up to Jack. Everyone seemed afraid of him but me. There would be many more times to observe this dynamic. Somehow, I knew that I had been roped into his zone of displeasure simply by being around, and by going to "that church".

Two weeks passed from that event and I looked forward to our date, but unfortunately, tragedy struck the day of the party, when the flu hit. Between runs to the bathroom to vomit, I would lie on my bed crying because I just knew that Mark would think that I was standing him up. Like a white knight to a damsel's aide came a friend, Helen, who attended the school of nursing with me. She was married and her children were nearly grown. Mark had grown up around them. My matchmaker, Helen, called Mark, and laid it on thick about how sick I was and how much I cared for him.

An hour later, my roommate brought me a card and a penlight flashlight. Inside the card, he had written "to the light of my life." That was such a sweet and understanding gesture. I was relieved that he understood, and that our friend had preserved our relationship.

CHAPTER TWELVE

THE 1812 OVERTURE

Spring came in like a lamb. The elm, cottonwood, and cherry trees were beginning to bud out and the scent of tulips and daffodils began to fill the air. Mark and I walked out the doors of the blonde brick church into a sunny day. We walked across the street to my blue 62 Chevrolet Bellaire. After I climbed into the car, Mark stood by the driver's side door staring down at the ground and began to kick the front tire.

"Ah-ah Diana?" Mark said quietly.

"Yea?"

"I-I love you."

This was followed by a long pause and I felt very uncomfortable.

"Mark, this is sudden. Don't you think we should talk about this later?

"Oh, okay."

"How about meeting me at Wesley's Chapel at about five this afternoon? Okay? I need time to think.

85

"Yea, sh-sure."

"I'll see you later then."

On my way back to the nursing school dorm, I was wondering how to break it to him that it was infatuation. He couldn't actually love me. We had known each other for a year and a half, but had just really started dating recently in earnest. Stuttering and his family's response to it had made him very shy. Asking me out had been very difficult for him. In spite of that, love was a huge leap in this relationship.

Mark and I sat on the cold granite bench outside the carved stone chapel. We sat in silence for a long time. I initiated the conversation.

"This is infatuation, Mark. It's just too soon to call it love." Mark sat with his head bowed in silence.

"I want to keep dating you, though. I really like you. Is that alright?" I asked hoping not to crush him. I felt bad that perhaps I had misled him as to my intention.

He nodded, and after another period of silence, we rose and walked back to the front lobby of the dorm hand in hand, where we said good-bye for the day.

Dating continued two to three days a week. Trying on hats at Sheplers Clothing Store one night, while laughing at each other, followed by a bowl of chili, was our typical fare. Another date took us to the park one sunny afternoon to sit on a blanket as we talked about nothing and everything. Suddenly, I saw a dandelion disappear underground.

"Did you see that?" I asked.

"Wh-wh-what?"

"Watch that dandelion."

"What am-m I watching for? "

"You'll know it when you see it."

With barely a beat between words, it happened again. Some mole was having a meal, and we laughed loud and long. Having someone wait while he stuttered, without interrupting or speaking for him, opened him up to share more and more. He told me that his family didn't know that he had a sense of humor, but I did. I felt privileged seeing sides of him that others had missed. He was a diamond in the rough.

Two weeks passed, and Mark met me downstairs at the front lobby of the dormitory for another date. I came down the stairs dressed in my pale pink and beige, princess-waist dress with a beaded choker, and my white dress shoes. Mark's face lit up as I entered the lobby. I smiled back, knowing that I had impressed him just the way I had hoped I would.

We prepared to leave for the St. Patrick's Day dance held by St. Joseph Hospital. Mark worked as an orderly there. Upon exiting the school, we walked across the parking lot to his blue 70 Pontiac Tempest, named "Go-fish", according to the license plate. Neither of us were very good dancers, but we got caught up in the bunny hop led by a heart surgeon we both knew. Mark snagged a green shamrock for me and we sat watching the ongoing dance.

At the end of the night, he drove me to the parking lot in front of the school of nursing. We sat in silence for quite a while letting the moment build. I had seen Mark in a whole different light this night. He was more relaxed and self-confident among his peers from the hospital, and I was having an epiphany.

"Mark, I thought you were infatuated with me when you told me that you loved me, but I must admit, I see it now, and I love you, too," I said very quietly, looking down into my lap. I felt my face flush warm with embarrassment and at the same time a feeling of happiness.

He smiled the smile of one who had been vindicated. This led to more conversation and finally it occurred to me that I didn't know what this love would mean. Where would we go from here?

"Mark, I'm going to be finishing school in the next few weeks, and I need to know whether to seek a job here in town, or go elsewhere to look for work." I realized that our relationship had reached a new level and I had no idea what we would do now. Without a pause for reflection or discussion, Mark said, "Will you marry me?"

As quickly as he asked it, I replied almost automatically. "Yes, I will."

I paused, and took a deep breath and swallowed hard. "I guess I'll look for work here," I said and I leaned toward Mark for a kiss.

We kissed for a while and then we discussed our future plans into the late-night hours. Finally, I asked

Mark the time, and realized I had better get inside before the dorm mother came looking for me. I exited the vehicle and went skipping for the door. I wanted to toot my horn to the second floor of the dorm, but I realized that I didn't have an engagement ring. The proposal had been spur of the moment, so I would wait for one before I broadcast much.

Upon arriving home at his parent's house after this momentous decision, Mark entered the front door with a large smile on his face, but he was greeted by his father who had stayed up waiting for him, and the smile evaporated.

"Where have you been so late?" Jack, Mark's father, asked while sitting in the living room in his blue recliner.

"I got en-engaged to Diana tonight!" he nearly crowed.

"Do you have to marry her?"

"No. Noth-nothing like that," Mark replied with emphasis.

"I can get someone to get you out of it, if you want."

"No, it's fine," Mark said firmly. "I love her."

"You get to bed, and we will see about this tomorrow," Jack growled.

In spite of his father's displeasure, dating continued much as before. At the end of each evening, we would discuss our education, mine to finish at Wesley, and his to decide what he wanted to do with the bachelor of science degree that he already had. He had studied fish in college and wanted to get his master's degree, but no funding had been available. In spite of our talk of a life together, still no ring manifested itself. Patience is not a strong quality with young women wishing for some binding token of their promise of marriage.

Dates came and went. Resorting to pointing at my fourth finger of the left hand, I finally got the idea across.

"Oh, you wa-want an engage-gagement ring?" He said having a moment of insight. "Do-do you want a pearl?"

"No, I was thinking of something more traditional."

"H-how about I let you know when I get it."

"Please, don't tell me. I want it to be a surprise. I want it to be romantic."

"Romantic? Okay, I'll do my best."

Time passed and no ring appeared, but he was very attentive, dropping off small gifts from time to time such as a single red rose or little lemons with faces drawn on them (from a talk about things I liked to eat). One day, he asked me if I wanted to go to one of the riverside parks along the Arkansas River for a picnic the next day. The spring weather was warm, but not hot, and the skies were clear with scattered soft rounded clouds. The park would be green and a real break from the dorm.

Next day, in the late afternoon, Mark picked me up for the picnic. There was no ring in sight. Driving north and west from the school, we found ourselves in a park separated from the river by a high hill. Pink and orange began to streak across the sky as the sun was beginning to set. The air was heavy with humidity and the smells of blossoming plants. Mark parked the "Gofish". He climbed out of the front seat, opened the trunk, and brought out strips of wood, a couple of nails, a few metal washers, and a hammer. Walking down a pathway, we came to the edge of a large pond.

"I thought we could b-build boats like you did as a kid on the f--farm."

"Oh, you mean the ones that my cousins and I played with in the cow trough? Okay, I guess." I was trying to follow what he had in mind, impressed that he remembered the story.

After pounding for a few moments, he launched the first boat out onto the pond. A metal washer was around the nail that held the boat together. Wafting through the air was the sound of the Wichita Symphony Orchestra playing the 1812 overture. That was when I remembered that it was the river festival that evening. The orchestra was playing downtown a short distance away, on the grounds in front of Century 2. About that time, a very large gold Koi breached the surface near the boat, which nearly turned it over. An alarming thought flashed through my mind. That wasn't a metal washer on that boat. It was my engagement ring!

"Mark, that's my ring! That fish will sink it to the bottom of that pond and we'll never see it again!"

Mark launched himself into the pond and grabbed the ring from the flimsy boat.

"Are you sur-prised?" he asked, walking out of the water.

"Surprised? You could say so," I said with a grin as I flung my arms around his neck.

We listened to the orchestra music locked in an embrace. As Mark prepared to slide the ring on my finger, cannons began to fire for that portion of the 1812 overture, and at the same time, fireworks filled the sky. Timing is everything, it is said. Mark had wonderful timing that night. We kissed and held each other, taking in the moment.

CHAPTER THIRTEEN

ADVENTURES

After the adventure of my engagement at the park, I believed that my life would be filled with exploits and fun as Mark's pent-up enthusiasm was finally released. My fiancé was still very quiet but also full of humor. He had found somebody to listen and accept him, and I had found the same.

I made the inevitable phone call to my parents. Mark and I had decided on a Saturday in October for our wedding. Before I dialed, though, I felt my heart race, my throat was dry, and my palms were moist. My parents would want to know all about Mark, and my dad could be hard to please.

"Well, I want to meet this young man," Dad said gruffly.

"I haven't heard much about him," Mom stated. I wanted them to appreciate Mark the way that I did and so I began to make a case for him.

"He's a lot like your dad, Mom. He's quiet but he is also witty. I think you'll like him. We met at church and plan to be married there. He's handsome, too."

"I'm coming to Wichita this weekend. I'd sure like to meet him," Dad announced. As soon as he said that, I wondered how that meeting would go and what Mark would think of my dad. My dad was coarse and outspoken and I worried that might scare Mark a little unless I forewarned him.

"I have to work, so I can't make it," Mom informed me. She worked six days a week, but dad was off every weekend. I was so proud of Mark that I certainly wanted both my parents to meet him. Mom balanced Dad out. I was disappointed she couldn't join him.

As soon as I got off the phone with my parents, I called Mark and asked him to come over. Mark and I met in the front lobby of the dormitory, and I took him into the formal sitting room across from the front desk.

With a serious look on my face I took his hands and leaned forward to say, "Now, Mark, I want you to know that my dad is coming here on Saturday. He wants to meet you."

Mark nodded. "Do you think he'll like me? I mean, what will he do if he doesn't like me? You told me that he had a lot of high-powered rifles." I had to look for a second to see that Mark was teasing.

"He won't do anything. He's met Cheryl's boyfriends before, and he behaved himself just fine."

Mark nodded again. "I sure hope we get along." Now, I could see that he really was nervous. Maybe I was making a bigger deal about this than I needed to.

"You'll do fine. I love you and so will he." I embraced him and gave him a kiss.

On Saturday evening, just as the sun set in pinks, oranges, and gold, Dad arrived. He had called me when he got into Hays, the halfway point, so I could have Mark at the dorm to meet him. Mark was apprehensive. He kept folding and unfolding a napkin.

"Don't worry," I said to him. "It'll only last a few hours."

"A lot can happen in a few hours," he replied.

I put my arms around him and said, "Remember, the most important person's opinion is mine, and I already think you're great."

Dad entered the dorm carrying two of Chris's oil paintings. I'd asked him to bring them along so I could put them up in my dorm room. Dad was very proud of Chris's ability to paint, and he bragged about them to Mark as he handed them to him. Mark gripped them like his life depended on it. I expected to see his fingerprints in them later. One of them was a lively orange, red, and yellow rooster, a copy of one by Van Gough, and it looked as if it might crow at any time. The other was a bowl of daisies which she had textured to give them depth.

We planned a meal at the hospital and walked to the school of nursing from the first floor of the dorm, followed the winding hallways, which took us to the hospital proper. Dad bragged to Mark that I would soon be an R.N. and asked me questions about how school was going until we came to the employee cafeteria. Mark and I showed him how to retrieve food and beverages, and Dad and I sat ourselves down to eat and visit while Mark held the paintings. I asked him if he wanted something, but he shook his head and said he'd already eaten. My guess was that nerves had made him lose his appetite.

"So, you're about done with school, here, right?" Dad asked while looking down at his plate.

"Yep, I made it. I graduate at the end of May. Here, let me get the invitation for you and Mom, and then I have one for Grandma, too," I said as I dug the invitations out of my purse. "Please tell grandma thank you for her help getting here."

"Say, Mark, you seem like a nice young man. What do you do for a living?"

"Oh, Mr. Middleton, right now I am working as an orderly at St. Joseph's Hospital here in town. I'm thinking of going back to school for something more substantial."

"Well, you ought to be a nurse like Diana, here. I tell all my friends what a fine school this is. Where do you live?"

"For now, I live with my folks, but I am going to be getting an apartment in a couple of weeks. Af-f-ter we are married, we both can live there. I helped Diana find an ap-p-artment behind my grandparents' house. She and her friend Nancy are going to move there before her graduation ceremony."

"That was nice of ya. Seems like you're already looking after each other pretty good," Dad said with a smile.

After Dad and I finished with ice cream, we walked back to the dorm. Dad paused at the doors and turned to Mark with a large smile and offered his hand. Quickly, Mark handed me the paintings and shook Dad's hand vigorously. I imagined Dad would have to wipe Mark's sweat off his palm when he got out the door.

"Nice to meet ya, Mark," Dad said. I gave Dad a peck on the cheek and he smiled and nodded his head in approval.

"See ya, Dad," I chirped and out the doors he went for the six-hour drive home. Dad had found out what he had come to Wichita for, and I'd gotten what I needed, his blessing.

"You passed, Mark," I said as I handed the frames back to him and patted him on the back. He gave a heavy sigh and smiled.

"Did I?" he asked. "Thank goodness." And then after a few seconds, "What should I do with these pictures?"

I took them off his hands and ran upstairs to put them in my room. We spent the rest of the evening talking about our future.

When graduation from Wesley finally arrived that May, Mark, my parents, and my sisters attended the ceremony at a large Methodist church in downtown Wichita. I was happy to finally walk up the red-carpeted aisle in the huge sanctuary and step up to Dean D., shake her hand, and receive my diploma.

I knew that nursing state boards would soon follow. I had to move out of the dormitory and would now rent the little house behind Mark's adopted grandparents' house. My first job would be in surgical intensive care and it would start in three weeks. Not much time for a break between graduation and my new position. Only two weeks before I had to hit the ground running, my parents invited us on a short trip to the Rocky Mountains so that I could at least feel like I had some kind of proper celebration.

My family often took treks to the Rockies since they were just 200 miles from Goodland. This time, my sisters would join my parents as well as a friend of Dad's, Jim. Cheryl, my oldest sister, would be bringing her step-son and her own little boy who was just learning to walk. Mark loved the Rockies and had gone fishing there with his dad several times, so he was excited to join us.

Up until now, Mark had seen my father as a happy and enthusiastic person, and he felt comfortable with him. But I knew that on this trip Mark would see the other side of my dad, and I was curious about how he would handle that.

We drove all day with stops only for necessities, and by evening when we finally stopped, we were at a campsite in the middle of the woods. The wind wafted gently through the trees, and a stream gurgled beyond the campsite. The fresh scent of the pines and the quiet delighted me. I had always loved the mountains and woods. We were far from other people or the sounds of towns, and nature was soothing for jostled nerves.

Dad was tired after driving through the mountains all day and he was barking and cursing and wasn't concerned about anyone's opinion of him. Like so often before while I was growing up, mom, my sisters and I jumped at the crack of his verbal whip trying to placate him. Mom worked quickly fixing supper while I made coffee for him. Unfortunately, as usual, our efforts did nothing to calm his temper.

I was embarrassed and frustrated and took a short hike to the cars parked up the hill from the campsite just to get out of ear shot of Dad, or I knew I was going to say something which would make everything worse. Within a few minutes, I heard no more yelling. It was totally quiet. I turned around to see all my family, including my new fiancé, standing in a circle with their heads bowed in prayer. Those who knew my family would have called this a miracle, and, I learned later, it had been brought about by Mark. I was right about him being like my mother's dad. Mark was a mediator. Dad would never cease yelling and cursing unless he respected someone. I knew it was not easy earning that respect. I also knew that a home with Mark would be a peaceful one, which is what I had always wanted.

Upon our return from our short breather in the mountains, I started my first real nursing job. I was considered a GN (graduate nurse) until my state board results came in. That took two months. I had bit off more than I could chew by taking a position in surgical intensive care. This was a major trauma hospital of over 800 beds, and the unit I was working was the most critical of the units in it. I had been too sure of myself when I graduated, but soon discovered how much I didn't know. It was terrifying most of the time as I helped care for open heart patients, craniotomies, and multiple traumatic injuries. I learned to manage respirators and chest tubes, and inter-cranial screws, and much, much more.

As I worked at SICU, Mark worked as an orderly at another hospital. On each spare day and moment, we would take care of a myriad of details for the wedding on our own. My parents would not be helping or paying. We were driven to near exhaustion.

Five months after my graduation, Mark and I were preparing for our wedding day. Dad again put my patience to the test. The plan was for me to get ready at the apartment that Mark and I had rented, put on my wedding dress, and let my sister do my hair and make-up before my dad arrived to take me to the church. My brother-in-law and my dad disappeared without a word, and were late getting to the apartment for the trip to the church. Three o'clock would soon be here and I was worried. I needed to get to the church for wedding photos and both of them were to be in them. At the last moment, in they walked.

"Where were you?" I yelled from the top of the stairs in Mark's apartment as I stood in my wedding dress.

"We were shopping for a rifle," Dad said lifting it up like some prize.

"On my wedding day?" I was livid. "Oh, men." My blood boiled and my temper peaked, but I held in my anger. We needed to get to the church without an argument. There was no time to spare.

We arrived at the church just in time and took family pictures. Afterwards, when I stood outside the wooden swinging doors that opened into the sanctuary, hearing the music we had picked out, I had a moment of feeling the hefty weight of this decision. How well did I know Mark? Was I really ready to spend the rest of my life with him? I had the questions that any serious person would have before they walked down the aisle, but I also knew that I was leaving behind a house filled with conflict and choosing to spend my life with a kind and gentle man.

The wedding march began, I paused, took a deep breath and marched through those doors. I met Mark at the top of the aisle and took his arm. My parents followed us, just as his parents followed them, and then the bridesmaids and groomsmen. We walked down the right aisle, where white silk bows adorned the pews. A candelabra was ablaze with long white tapers and maroon flowers cascaded down. Above the rostrum on the back wall was a huge stain glass picture of Christ kneeling in the Garden of Gethsemane. My doubts passed completely away as I looked at Mark's broad smile.

Elder Burl Allen officiated and reminded us that we were taking an oath before God. From above, in the choir loft, came the musical version of "Make me an Instrument of Thy Peace," which we had sung together in choir before we became engaged. The words were a prayer from St. Francis of Assisi. That song made all the difficulties of the day melt away into an awe of God's Spirit.

Burl turned to Mark and invited him to speak his vows.

"Diana, with this ring I pledge you my life, my love, my all. From this day something great and good will happen with us as we become a testimony of God's great love."

I read Elizabeth Barrett Browning's famous poem, "How do I love thee? Let me count the ways."

When all the vows were said and the last prayer prayed, Burl presented us to the congregation as Mr. and Mrs. Mark Dodds. And so our life together began.

CHAPTER FOURTEEN

WHERE DO WE BEGIN?

The Pontiac rolled down the street, but to others on the street, it sounded more like a Sherman tank. Of course, the car was decorated with graffiti and two strings of cans bounced behind. The rocks in the hub caps gave the illusion of a tank. Upon arriving at our apartment, I slipped into the building to grab our bags, while Mark took off the hub caps and emptied out the stones. From there, we drove to the interstate, and headed south to Oklahoma. We stopped at a car wash on the way and removed the majority of the decorations. Both Mark and I had slept very little the night before the wedding, and now as we wound down the grey asphalt road, toward a state-run lodge, the fatigue began to take its toll. In the rear-view mirror, red and blue lights began flashing. Mark pulled over. I was lying with my head on his lap, and sat up while the highway patrol officer cautioned Mark about weaving on the road. It was time to stop for the night. Our first night together would be at a motel halfway to our goal.

The reality of being free to love completely filled us with sexual desire. We poured ourselves into one another, as we had longed to do. The warmth we then felt matched the degree of our commitment to one another. Resting my head on his chest, we talked about our dreams for the future. I wanted children, but we both knew that until Mark could use his education for more than being an orderly, it would be difficult to do. For now, there would be birth control and we would wait.

The honeymoon lasted for 5 days, and then it was time to go back to Wichita, and begin the business of actually living a life together. Mark had chosen to go into nursing. We had often shared our common experiences relative to caring for people in the hospital, and he had decided that working as a nurse was a good use of his degree in biology. In spite of that degree, he had courses such as human growth and development, human anatomy and physiology (he had studied every other type of A&P), and sociology that he had to take to match the pre-requisites for Wesley, which was the school that he had chosen.

Over the next year, I worked first at a surgical intensive care for 5 months, then for 7 months as a charge nurse on a medical-surgical floor. Finally, I found my niche at a coronary care unit. Mark worked at the hospital as an orderly, and from time to time, we would be involved with the same patient and could visit for a few rushed minutes. I was the bread winner for the family, as Mark was taking college classes and working.

For our first Christmas together, I asked the familiar question about what he wanted for his gift. He said he wanted me, which was not a big help and so we gave each other what we called foundation gifts. The clothes hamper we needed, or the underwear. On Christmas morning, I sat on the floor next to the Christmas tree with a bow on my head, which made him laugh. We had very little, but it didn't seem like very little, because we had each other.

There were times when I would feel the pressure of being the main provider, and of working in a field where there were very few mentors to teach me the ropes. There was a nursing shortage and many experienced nurses had retired. When I finally found a job in CCU, I found mentors who taught me heart rhythms and cardiac protocols. I was able to use my limited experience and build on it. There were many nights with tears after particularly difficult days, but Mark was always there to comfort me.

CHAPTER 15

WHIRLWIND: I

I have come to see difficult times in life as whirling dervishes that turn us around until we can't see the road of life ahead of us. Struggling along as a human being is life.

Pregnancy is one of those events in living that can be glorious or not. Every woman who becomes pregnant is risking her life, and her future life as well. Three years passed with Mark and I holding our breath, waiting to have a child, until Mark was done with nursing school. I had lifted and carried the yoke of primary wage earner for nearly three years, and it made me ready to take on a more traditional parental role. Calculating to the nth degree of time, we planned for the child for which we had dreamed. We had become acquainted with an OB/GYN before we got married, and he had helped us with birth control measures. Now, finally, I went to him and prayed that I would not need that birth control for a while.

"Diana, you are pregnant," Dr. H. announced after a thorough examination.

"Really? That's wonderful!" I pulled my feet out of the metal stirrups on the exam table. I had never had regular periods, so I needed to be sure.

"Are you having any nausea?" Dr. H. inquired.

"No, I feel really good, except a bit tired," I replied.

"I am going to need some blood work and a urine sample before you go."

I crossed the office hallway to the bathroom carrying the specimen cup and I don't think my feet touched the floor. I felt like I had won the lottery.

After Dr. H. diagnosed me with anemia and prescribed iron and prenatal vitamins, I went to Mark who waited in the reception area. I flung myself around his neck and announced the news. Mark gave me a welcome and reassuring hug. I would need to notify work of my due date in May.

In spite of working full-time as a nurse, I emoted happiness. As I progressed through the pregnancy, I began to resemble the Goodyear blimp. I allowed one of the cardiologists that I worked with, to shoot a photo of me in a side view, and I didn't care. I was content and my co-workers said they had never seen me so happy.

A week after Mark graduated from nursing school, I was in the obstetrics department. I was 2 ½ weeks overdue, and my obstetrician, Dr. H., decided to check my baby's maturity in-utero, by doing an amniocentesis that showed that the baby was full term. In the process of doing the amniocentesis my water broke. I was induced with a Pitocin drip and went into vigorous labor. With a fetal monitor wrapped around my large abdomen, each contraction's strength and the baby's heart rate could be tracked. The strength of the contractions were off the chart shortly after they began and I was assured that I should make quick progress. We knew from an ultrasound that we were having a boy and we had already picked the name of Patrick. Patrick's heart rate dropped briefly after each labor pain, and then rebounded back up again in between pains, which is what normally happens in labor as the placenta is squeezed with each contraction.

After six hours, Patrick was not making any progress down the birth canal and it was taking longer and longer for his heart rate to rebound, until it began reaching the point that he was not fully rebounding. Dr. H. informed me that Patrick's head circumference and the diameter of my pelvic outlet was mismatched, which meant Patrick could not be born vaginally. Fortunately for me, they had already given me an epidural block, so that I was numb from the waist down. I was prepared for a Caesarean section. During my labor, Mark had trouble staying with me. He was very anxious and took many breaks going out to see his parents who were in the waiting room, but the labor nurse had stayed at my bedside every minute. An adventure in the operating room would become one of those swirling and spinning whirling dervishes.

I rolled down the hallway, and Mark settled himself down and followed me into the operating room. The operating room was cold, and the operating bed colder still. With attachments like a heart monitor to my chest, oxygen blowing up my nose, and a sticky cold grounding pad for the electric cautery, which is used to control bleeding with searing electric current, attached to my leg, I was prepared quickly and efficiently for major surgery. Cloth drapes were arranged to ensure a separation of my head from my torso. Each arm was put on a board, one for the intravenous catheter and the other for a blood pressure cuff. Finally, I looked like I was resting on a cross, unable to see or move, except for my head.

One of the nurses had assisted Mark to change into operating scrubs and shoe covers and seated him on a rolling exam chair, next to my head. This was unheard of in 1978, but since Mark had passed through this department as a student nurse, they made an exception. From his vantage point, he could see the heart monitor for our son. Mark watched the monitor carefully as instruments were put in their proper place, and Dr. H. entered after scrubbing, gowned and gloved.

My husband suddenly shouted, "The baby's heart rate just dropped off!"

The harried staff scrambled and in the background I heard the circulating nurse say, "Call the Newborn Intensive Care Unit and prepare for an emergency delivery!"

Panic began its work as I struggled against the oxygen mask being placed over my face. I thought that they were putting me under general anesthesia and I would wake to a dead baby.

"It's oxygen, Diana, don't struggle!" Mark pleaded.

My ears strained to hear, as the doctor worked feverishly to extricate my son from his fleshy tomb in the uterus. The doctor handed the circulating nurse his lifeless, limp blue body.

"We have an Apgar of 2," the scrub nurse called out, using a scale from 0-10 rating a baby's ability to survive, to alert the doctor of the baby's condition as he continued the surgery. Tears rolled down my cheeks and a helpless feeling enveloped me, because I knew how critically low that Apgar was. The nurse suctioned out his nose and mouth and gave him stimulation to help him breathe.

When I finally heard a lusty cry, the nurse chirped, "Apgar is an 8 at 5 minutes."

Finally, I could breathe. Mark sighed and smiled.

Medications surged through my system and a certain giddiness began.

"What's that tugging I feel?" I queried the doctor.

"I'll throw in more stitches if you aren't happy," he joked.

I laughed to myself as the relief flooded over me completely and the swirling dervish ceased into smoothness.

My son, Patrick, was thriving by the time the nurse brought him to me in the recovery room. I locked eyes with Patrick as he nuzzled and finally began nursing at my breast. He had fine, almost white-blonde, hair, which made him look nearly bald. His head was perfectly round, as C-section babies normally are. Patrick reached out and grasped my finger, and I knew that I would do anything for him. Out in the hallway, Mark carried the news of his son's arrival to his parents and our good friend, Cindy. Cindy had been asked to be his godmother, and she became so excited that she picked Mark up and twirled him around in a circle.

I was transferred to the post-operative obstetric unit. As the numbness of the epidural subsided, I was started on Percocet for pain. Mark had called my parents and my sisters to notify them that Patrick was here. Mom then called me.

"Diana, honey, how are you doing?" Mom asked.

"I'm tired, but I'm comfortable right now. Did Mark tell you that I had a C-section?"

"Yes, he filled us in on what happened."

"Mom, they are keeping me here for 4 to 5 days, so you don't need to come up here until I get home."

"Diana, I am so sorry. Mr. W. won't give me the time off."

"What? I thought you had vacation time coming."

"Well, Mr. W. had promised that I could come there on my vacation time, but now he says it's too close to wheat harvest. Since I work in the parts department, I have to be here if the farmers need last minute parts for their combines or tractors. I think there is plenty of time before harvest, but he's the boss."

Warm salty tears formed at the corners of my eyes, but I knew that Mom was trapped. She paid most of the bills and couldn't afford to lose her job. Dad paid the house payment and kept the rest of his money in a roll to impress people.

"Dad is going to bring Chris there to help, ok?"

"Okay Mom, thanks." The thought of Chris being my only help at home did not fill me with much hope. She rarely if ever helped Mom around the house. I resigned myself to the news.

"Love ya honey. You get some rest now." I hung up the phone and drifted off to sleep.

Toward the end of my 3rd post-op day, I was medicated for pain, and fell into a deep sleep. I thought I was hearing voices in the hallway, and they sounded like my mom and Mark's half-sister, Susan. I tried to open my eyes, so I could go out and speak to them, but was unable to. When I was finally able to open them, I went out to the hallway and found no family there. When I asked the nurses at the nurse's station about my visitors, I was informed that there had been no visitors that afternoon. My nurse determined that it was time to stop the Percocet. I must have dreamed that I heard their voices.

Upon discharge, the usual insomnia-laden time with a newborn began: up every two hours on average for breast feeding. I proceeded to try to be the perfect parent. I changed Pat's diaper and held him close to me, rocked him, and sang him my favorite songs as lullabies.

By the time he finally would relax and allow me to put him into bed and stay asleep, I could sleep perhaps an hour before he was up again to repeat the cycle. There was laundry to do and whatever housework I could manage.

Mark, as a brand new RN, was working 11pm-7am shifts. These took up his entire night and some hours beyond his shift, as Mark too was a perfectionist. At some point he had to get sleep if he was going to continue to work. Changing diapers is one of the things you learn in nursing school, so Mark made no excuses. He would be up in the evening after he had slept through the day, which gave me some time to rest. Chris sat in the corner of the living room and drew constantly. When I asked for her help with Patrick, she informed me that he was not her son. So, instead of getting help, I had received someone else to care for. She left for home a week after arriving, so I was on my own. Susan, Mark's half sister, sat with Patrick for a couple of hours one day, and I got some much-needed rest.

I insisted on breastfeeding without using a bottle to supplement, so Mark could not help me there. We worked together as parents, but this left little time for sleep. We were young and felt we would always be able to maintain ourselves.

As time passed, a persistent fatigue pervaded my day. There was also sadness, and a helpless feeling, for which I could not find a reason. I knew that most women got depressed after childbirth, but mine continued on as weeks slowly passed. It was as if I was looking up from a deep well. Everything I did felt like a great effort. It was like walking through molasses. I was discovering that depression is not just about mood, but energy as well.

After six weeks of this drill, I was completely drained. I felt in desperate need of sleep and more help then Mark could give me. The plan was to have my uncle come and bless Patrick, which was a sacrament of our church, but at the last minute I flew home to Goodland with Patrick to see my parents.

My father picked up Patrick and I at the little country airport in Goodland. My dad immediately took me to a café and got me pancakes. For the first time since I could remember, my father cut up my food for me and I ate without even looking up, as Dad entertained Patrick. My mother helped me put Patrick on the bottle and find a formula that would not cause him colic. Using the bottle to feed Pat when I wanted to sleep helped the physical part of my state. The C-section had been major surgery, and I finally felt as though I might heal from it. After a week of recovery, I flew home with Pat.

I returned to the same situation as before I left, except that I had help feeding Patrick so that I could get more rest. The sadness and lethargy remained. The pearl of wisdom regarding postpartum depression I had learned in school said that if it persisted for six weeks or more, the doctor should be notified, because it could be something serious. I would hopefully get some answers when I saw Dr. H. again for my six-week checkup.

CHAPTER SIXTEEN

WHIRLWIND: II

Preparing for a postoperative checkup gave me a sense of apprehension. Physically, I knew I was doing well, but emotionally I had continued to sink. I had tried to hang this depression on some event like one would hang a hat on a hook, because I could then fix the problem, but I couldn't find a reason for my feelings. I needed a life preserver and the doctor threw me one.

"You just need to get back with other adults," he said. "You need to go back to work."

That was it! I had a solution to this pervasive sadness that had plagued me. I asked my sister-in-law, Susan, if she could watch Patrick while I went to my alma mater, the medical center, which had the attached nursing school that both Mark and I had attended.

When I entered the nursing office, I was greeted with, "Where would you like to work?"

There was a nursing shortage in those days and you could walk into any hospital in the city and have a job.

Before I left the nursing office, I was signed up for a
week of orientation classes to prepare me for a job at the
facility. I felt invigorated and hopeful at last.

After being up half the night with Patrick, I showered
and changed and prepared for my first day of orientation. Susan, took over with Pat. I didn't think past the
day ahead of me. Like a thoroughbred prances with excitement at the thought of the race, I went to class.

Throughout the week, my mind became more and
more clear and vibrant. Each class built on the last, as
did my thought process. My mind responded like that
same racehorse to the urging jockey. My perceptions
seemed more acute. I began to anticipate what the instructors would say before they said it. My hand shot up
time after time, until I completely took over the classes.

By the end of the week, my mind was so filled with
thoughts that it was as if some fireman had turned on
a fire hose of inspiration in it. The thoughts were coming so quickly that my consciousness could not process
them all. I grabbed a streaking thought here and there
as I could which made the listener jump from subject
to subject without any connecting thoughts. The fatigue
was completely gone, although the time I spent up with
Patrick and keeping house had not changed. It was the
opposite of the depression I had experienced. I was elat-
ed and extremely optimistic about everything. It seemed
as though I had boundless energy. On the last day of
the week, I was stopping folks in the hallway explaining
God's plan for this hospital and its talented employees.

"The Holy Spirit will pour into each and every one of them and they will become the light on the hill!" I explained with much enthusiasm.

I was oblivious to the oddity I presented. My hair askew, snatches of thought jumping from here to there.

On the way home, on the last day of that week, as I turned the corner towards home, it became clear to me that I was the prophet of God. The delusions had begun.

"Mark, Mark wake up! God has chosen me to be his prophet," I yelled as I entered the house. A very tired and startled man roused from a sound sleep. I jabbered a hundred miles an hour, and I started making long distance calls. I spoke so quickly and jumped from here to there with my thoughts so frequently that my sister, Cheryl, could not follow me. The pressure to speak was overwhelming.

The more I spoke, the more disjointed my verbalizations became, and more bizarre. I sent my bewildered husband on some errand to spread "the word". Unsure of what was transpiring he left to do as I asked. I sat in a chair in front of a blank TV screen. Skeletons, like cartoon figures, danced across the screen and I was briefly mesmerized. As I looked to my right, I saw a knife floating in the air in the hallway leading to Pat's room, where he slept peacefully. Fortunately, my mind was drawn back to the dancing skeletons. My body was pounding fists on my mind trying to say how tired it was, but my mind, like a driver in a city where all the lights were green, raced hither and yon unimpeded.

Mark trudged in the door. His fatigue from working nights and caring for our son, and trying to follow my frenetic pace, began to tell on him. Pat cried the cry of the hungry, and dutifully, I strolled in the room. Like a robot, I changed his diaper and held him to my breast. Comforted, I handed him to Mark. The house was still, but my mind and body were not. As often as Patrick needed care, I gave it like a rote response.

On the phone again, I spoke to my parents with such a sense of urgency that they hung on every word as if it dripped from the mouth of God. I had never misled them in my life, so what I told them now somehow seemed plausible to them.

"You must come here, now."

"You will be accused of killing someone."

"The police will be looking for you."

"You must come, now."

"Drive slowly and carefully so you won't draw suspicion to yourselves." I told them all these various statements amongst other things.

Dutifully, they quickly prepared for the 300-mile journey to Wichita, and drove well within the speed limit and watched for police. The last they had seen me, I made sense and so they didn't seem to suspect anything wrong.

While their journey proceeded, I prepared a feast. I cooked everything I could find and arranged the dining room table like a welcome home dinner for what I perceived to be the prodigal son, my dad. I would turn my dad back to what I knew was his childhood faith. It never occurred to me that he wouldn't understand my purpose.

Towards morning, there was a knock at the door. Mark sat holding Pat. I greeted them quoting scripture, disheveled and loud. I led them to the kitchen, where I had food cooked and piled on every surface. With a forceful voice, I commanded my father:

"Get to your knees and worship God!"

Frightened by my manner, my father who normally would be yelling and commanding me, dropped to his knees. I was briefly jubilant. I stepped through the door-way of the kitchen, and set down like one would drop a sack of potatoes forcefully into the recliner in the front room. My father crawled to the side of the chair, and as I turned to look at him, his neck became a snake with his head turned toward my face. In fear, I covered my face with my hands."

"Diana, it's just me, Dad."

"No, get away!" I cried, refusing to move my hands and clinching my eyes together tightly."

"Elva?" Dad said turning to my mother.

"Honey, it's just me and Dad here. What can we do?"

"Just give her some space," Mark suggested and waved my parents over to talk about the situation out of my hearing.

After spending a few moments talking to Mark about what had been going on before they arrived, my parents called my sisters, Chris and Cheryl, who were in Washington State where Cheryl now lived. My parents were expected there for their vacation. After a short discussion, where my sister Cheryl suggested they stay and see if I needed their help, my parents decided that they would pack up and leave. They had a plane to catch in Denver and it was going to be a long trip to get there. Their vacation to the great northwest would go on without a hitch. They had already paid for the tickets after all. Years later, when I talked to my mother about what seemed like abandonment, she said:

"I thought you would be alright. You always seemed to manage. I was worried about you, but I didn't know what to do."

The downward spiral of events continued after my parents left. Pat slept the sleep of the unknowing and Mark tried to fathom this bizarre creature who rattled on unceasing. She was nothing like the wife he knew just 24 hours ago. Unfazed by my parent's exit, I continued in my own world. I asked Mark to find someone to administer the laying on of hands for healing for me. He left briefly.

After Mark drove away, another knock came at the door. A young man and his fiancée from our church, with whom I had worked as a camp nurse, were at the door. They were asking for some guidance as the young woman would be taking on that role. I tried to explain how it was done, but it made no sense to them. I pointed to a broken tape recorder on the table and told them that my 2-month-old son would talk to them through it. The young woman bolted for the door and ran to their car. The young man, who had known me for years, began backing to the door, asking my forgiveness. "I'm sorry, Diana. She doesn't know you," he said while giving me a sad soulful look. He exited the door and went to his fiancée who had locked herself in their car.

Unfazed by their exit, I continued in my own world. Soon, Mark came up the walk and onto the porch, followed closely by a member of the priesthood of the church, an elder we both had known since I arrived in Wichita for nursing school. For some reason it struck me as my ascension to Prophet. Mark managed to get me to again sit in the chair.

The elder that Mark had brought stood behind the chair and put drops of oil on my head from a small glass bottle. He laid his hands upon my head. Although this felt familiar, I continued to jabber on unimpeded.

"Shut up!" he said sternly.

I tried my best to cease the raging torrents of thoughts that plunged through my mind. My face flushed and small tears welled up in my eyes while the on-going speech became a whisper. As he prayed for me, I suddenly had a brief moment of clarity.

"You are sick. You need help," the voice said.

After the elder left, the words kept bobbing to the surface over and over. By this time, it was dark, and I was moving into 48 hours of uninterrupted talking. Mark had been taken by surprise by my behavior over the last 2 days, and had been at a loss as to how to get me help if I was not being cooperative. Finally, I felt the need for help as well. My diaphragm began to spasm from exhaustion, and I could get out only one word at a time.

"I—need—help."

Mark called his mother to come help take me to the hospital.

Fear gripped me as though I was about to die. My body was on the verge of collapse. I laid on the bed and whispered,

"Twent-y—th-ird—Psalm."

Mark opened the scriptures and read it to me as he waited for his mom. My mother-in-law arrived in her pajamas, coat, and curlers. I attempted to talk as we walked to the car, but it was not understandable.

Arriving at the emergency room entrance, Mark walked me into the ER. My mother-in-law held Patrick on her lap in the waiting room. In an exam room, it did not take the doctor long to see the deterioration I had undergone. He ordered anti-psychotic medication to be given to me in a shot. Mark stood and held my hand. Later, as they rolled me out of the room on the cart, I realized where I was going. It would be on the same psychiatric unit I had worked as a student. I was in the hospital where just 2 days before I had been preparing to work.

"Oh, God not this," I cried over and over as the lights on the ceiling passed overhead. A sense of shame and fear enveloped me. I was assisted into a bed on the psychiatric unit and the medication finally took hold as I drifted off to sleep.

After I was admitted, Pat was spirited away to his grandparent's house, and Mark returned to our home and Pat's nursery. He sat about tearing down the crib to move it to his parent's house. Then, the entire world crashed down on him. His wife was not his wife anymore. Her mind had taken a trip to an unknown shore. He was tearing down the crib that the two of us had assembled together just months before. As he sat in the middle of the floor, he began to quake and sobs came pouring out. He was caught up in a whirlwind and there was no discernible road ahead.

CHAPTER SEVENTEEN

THROUGH THE FOG

The fog of war is about the confusion of war and what can happen because of that confusion. Psychiatric units are also a fog when you've been psychotic. The first day that I awoke on the psychiatric floor at the medical center, it was definitely cloudy. After sleeping through the night, for the first time in a several days, the psychosis that had caused me to be admitted had decreased. Lack of sleep increases psychosis, so sleep had decreased it.

Warm sunlight began beaming into the room from a single window, which was opposite my hospital bed. Pink and light blue tinged the early morning sky as I awoke to the sound of a lab person quietly stepping into the room to draw blood from my roommate. After the technician made multiple attempts to get her blood, he finally left the room.

I returned to sleep for an hour or so and when I awoke, it was to a familiar face standing over me.

Evelyn, the nurse standing there, had graduated with me from nursing school . My face felt hot with embarrassment. My mind raced and I knew that I would not be able to control the onslaught. I pleaded over and over with Evelyn to take my blood pressure. My pressure was elevated which in my addled brain meant that I needed to be locked up for my own safety and the safety of those around me. Memories of the psychiatric patient I had cared for years ago flashed through my brain. I begged Evelyn to transfer me to the locked unit. The more she tried to tell me that it wasn't necessary, the more adamant I became. Relenting, she called my psychiatrist, who gave her permission to move me. I was placed in a wheelchair and rolled through the hallways to the sliding glass doors of the locked psychiatric unit.

Once the glass doors of the closed unit clicked shut behind me, I felt more at ease. When the mind feels out of control, it seeks control from the outside. The nurse on duty that day was named Karen. She recognized me from my time as a student. Petite, about five foot three, slender with blonde hair, she commanded the unit like someone twice her size.

I was sure Karen remembered a time when I was a student nurse and made a big mistake. I was allowed to retrieve a razor from my patient's drawer this particular day, so the patient could shave her legs during a bath, while I supervised. The other patients knew I was a student and when I unlocked the closet door where objects were kept that might injure a patient, hands appeared from everywhere to retrieve their items, which disappeared without supervision. That day, I found Karen as quickly as I could and informed her of the breach in protocol.

At nearly the same time, I was called to the front of the unit to sit with my instructor and recite the side effects for anti-psychotic medication which were as long as your arm. While trying to concentrate on my task, I heard a buzz and the glass doors slid open and a security guard in a riot helmet carrying a baton raced in and threw his baton and gun into the nurses' station where Karen waited. This routine continued until there were six guards. At that point, Karen came out of the station and followed the guards to a back room where a young man, about six-foot-tall, was threatening the rest of the patients with a rat tail comb. Soon the noise subsided as the guards put the young man in restraints and Karen medicated him with sedating medication. In spite of my poor performance as a student that day, her manner towards me this day was pleasant and professional.

Later that morning, Karen and I talked about what had gone on at home. She gave me medication, and I felt more in control of my thoughts. Early in that same afternoon, Mark came to visit. I cried when I saw him. We went to my room and left the door open, which was the rule. Mark sat on my bed and put his arm around my shoulder and I laid my head against his chest. I asked about Patrick, my newborn son. Mark assured me that his parents were caring for Patrick and that Pat was safe.

Mark was only able to stay with me for a few minutes because I was easily agitated at the time. He kissed me on the cheek and whispered good-bye. I started pacing after that, while energy began surging again. Karen came and gave me antipsychotic medication and lithium, which helped me regain some self-control.

My medication regimen was in high dosages to wrangle my psychosis down. The delusions subsided and the hallucinations were gone within the first 5 days. Breast-feeding was discontinued because of the medications I was on, which would pass through the breast milk to Patrick. Firm, tender breasts were a reminder that Patrick was not with me and it tore at my heart. My arms ached to hold him once again. Mark came back to visit me every day for a few minutes, and I spent the rest of my days waiting for those few morsels of time.

By the end of the first week in the hospital, I had been stable for a couple of days. Karen was cordial and encouraging about the progress I had made. Hallucinations and delusions had finally ceased. My experience began to feel like a terrible nightmare. The clearer my thinking became, the clearer my recollections became, and along with them came guilt and shame. In spite of Mark's support, there was the growing fear that I could lose Mark and Patrick forever.

I was to be taken care of by a different psychiatrist over the weekend than the one following my care during the week. Karen and the weekend doctor, Dr. R., had me go to my room where he would talk with me.

"Look at me. Do I look like the devil?" Dr. R. asked me, which was a reference to a hallucination that I had before I was admitted. Karen saw the look on my face as I realized that he knew nothing about how I had been the past couple of days. I so badly wanted to say, 'yes, you look like the devil to me,' but the look in Karen's eyes told me not to make a joke out of this.

"No, sir, you don't look like the devil." With that reassurance, he thought I was ready to be transferred back to the voluntary open unit.

I felt safe on the open unit this time, but the side effects of the medications began to become troublesome. When not being interviewed by staff and physicians, there really was not much to occupy my time. I tried to read, but it had become impossible because when holding books where I normally would hold them, the letters on the page would blur. Holding the same book out far enough that it wasn't blurry made it too far away to read. My vision had always been normal before this and so I was sure it was the medication that was doing this.

My handwriting also changed. My hands were stiff, and my usually flowing cursive turned to smaller and smaller scribbles. When not doing purposeful movements, my hands would have a fine tremor. My face felt stiff and I had to concentrate in order to smile. Pseudo-Parkinson's is the best analogy I could make for these side effects of the antipsychotics. Tremors, dry mouth, and constant urination became other issues caused by lithium, which added to the side effects of the anti-psychotic medication I already had, not counting the daily blood tests for it.

Discussing this with the nursing staff didn't provide me with any relief. I was not seen as a nurse at this point. I was a patient like everyone else on the unit, and somehow it felt like a slap in the face to have my concerns dismissed. I knew these were side effects that didn't need to be this severe, but I was helpless to do anything about them.

Dr. R. came to the voluntary unit and gave me a pass to go with Mark for three hours on the hospital grounds. Meandering around the hospital and the school of nursing, Mark and I were quiet for quite a while and then we began to discuss our vision of the future.

"I don't even know for sure what this was. What if I'm schizophrenic? What will we do? I won't be able to go back to work. What about me taking care of Patrick?"

"Diana, we don't know enough yet to make any decisions." Putting his arms around me, he pulled me in and whispered in my ear "We will get through this." We mulled over what had occurred and tried to reassure each other, but my fear remained. Upon returning to the psychiatric floor, I kissed Mark good-bye.

Monday, I was given psychological tests with well over five hundred questions to answer. I told the nursing staff that I couldn't read the questions, due to my visual changes, and asked if they could read them to me. They refused to help because they said that they didn't want to influence the answers. I got the impression each time that I asked for their help, that they thought I was trying to manipulate them in some way. Emotional problems don't make you manipulative. The realization dawned upon me that I was being judged by my diagnosis and not being seen as an individual.

Back in my room, my roommate, Tammy, had the same personality tests and she had the same side effect issues related to her vision as I did. I found out at that time that she had also had a postpartum psychotic event. We spent many hours squinting and moving the test pages various distances to try to make out the questions. "What do you think 139 says?" I asked. She would give me her version while I did the same on a different question of hers. How accurate this method of testing we were attempting could be was anyone's guess. Having someone else who was experiencing this condition helped me feel a little more normal.

That evening, Dr. H., my OB/GYN, came to see me. When we had arrived in the ER two weeks prior, Mark gave the ER physician Dr. H.'s name. Together, the two doctors helped find a psychiatrist to admit me. He and I had bonded over my pregnancy, delivery, and my postpartum visit. Now, we talked on a superficial level for a short time about the weather and hospital food and finally I asked the question that I had been too afraid to ask.

"Do you think this will ever happen again?"

His reply dropped like a bomb. "You'll have this problem for the rest of your life."

Silence was my only reply at first. He turned, and exited my room and went down the hall. There was an eruption rising in me and then it exploded. I chased him down the hall and yelled, "How do you know? You don't know me!"

He kept walking. I returned to my room with tears stinging my red face. Denial is a safe harbor when reality is too much to take in. I laid down on my bed, and turned to the wall to ponder his answer through the night.

Tuesday morning, after a two-week admission, my psychiatrist was satisfied that I was stable and could go home. Finally, I received the dreaded yet anticipated diagnosis. Manic-depression was that diagnosis. The post-partum psychosis was actually my first manic event. I would be sent to an outpatient mental health clinic in two weeks, and until then, I would continue on my current medication. The energy that had driven this mania had sapped my strength, and exhaustion weighed heavy on me. Sleep would be a balm.

My first week home after discharge, at our rented house, was mostly sleep. When I was awake, I felt sad and empty. When a person has received a psychiatric diagnosis, they become perpetually observed lest the disease raises its ugly head again. Mark began to fear that I was getting seriously depressed. He knew that depression followed mania. What he could not know was that this was also grief for the life that would never be the same again. I could never tell myself again that I was not capable of being mentally ill. Never in my life did I expect to find myself here. Mark talked to my psychiatrist about his concern about my social withdrawal and change in sleep habits, and the doctor ordered an antidepressant be added to my regimen.

Within three days of starting the antidepressant, my mood was more upbeat and I was ready to spend time with Patrick. I drove the few short blocks to Mark's parent's house, where Patrick was still living. Shortly after coming through their front door, I prepared to hold Pat by removing my sweater. Patrick had changed over the three weeks that I had been away from him. He looked at me with his beautiful blue eyes but didn't smile at me like he had done before. I felt a deep sadness at the thought that he might have felt abandoned when I went to the hospital. I took him to Dorothy's recliner, which doubled as a rocking chair. Pat began to get fussy and began to arch his back and look around. I checked his diaper and it was clean and dry so I concluded that he needed his bottle.

Dorothy heated up a bottle on the stove for me and gave it to me. I checked the warmth of the formula on my wrist, and began to feed him. After I laid Patrick down in his crib to sleep, I went into the kitchen, where Jack and Dorothy, Mark's parents, were making up more bottles for him. Jack began to instruct me on how to do it, as if I didn't know how. The fact that I had done it before I was sick and taught them both how to do it didn't seem to matter. I was mentally ill, not incompetent.

I felt turmoil bubbling up inside me in relation to who I was now. I needed to explain it to Dorothy, as I saw her as the more sympathetic of Mark's parents. I needed her to see that I had a disability but it was one that could not be seen, because there was no wheelchair or white cane. I wanted her to know that in spite of this disability I needed to do all that I was capable of doing. Dorothy listened politely, but did not reply. Following her into her bedroom, which was up a short hallway from the kitchen, I said,

"After all, Mark saw a mental health counsellor when he was 18 years old. He told me about it when we were dating one another."

"That's a lie!" Jack spouted from the kitchen.

"No, it's not. Mark told me," I said in disbelief.

"It's not true!" he insisted.

Unbeknownst to me, Dorothy called Mark at work and asked him to come to their home as soon as possible because she was worried that I was getting sicker.

I felt confused by Jack's declaration, because I knew what Mark had told me, and that I was not lying. I had never been called a liar before, and I felt anger and sorrow that Jack would accuse me unfairly. Being mentally ill didn't make you a liar. I wandered back into the kitchen, and noticed Jack's blood pressure medication on the counter. Mark and I had looked up this medicine for Jack once when we were first married, and we were both surprised to find that it was what is called an MAO inhibitor. It seemed odd, as this type of medication mixed with the wrong foods could cause a severe spike up in blood pressure, which could lead to death. We had told him about it, but it appeared he was still using it. MAO inhibitors were also the first drugs used as antidepressants.

At that moment, I launched into the choppy sea of delusions once again. In my mind, two plus two was five. Jack was on an MAO inhibitor, which in my mind meant he was on an antidepressant, which meant depression, which meant he was mentally ill and suicidal. This was psychotic logic. I felt vindicated because I was sure that Jack was mentally ill like me.

I walked out the back door and into the yard following after Jack. Mark drove up in the driveway and proceeded to the backyard where he heard my voice. I walked up to Jack who was seated at a picnic table and tried to convince him to go to the hospital with me. I was sure he was in danger of harming himself.

"You know nobody loves you more than Dorothy and I," he said.

My experience with Jack's disapproval and his carefully worded snipes that left a person bleeding before they could fully defend themselves had proven just the opposite to me. I had no delusions about his dislike of me.

"My parents love me more than you do," I said firmly.

"Well, if they loved you so much, they wouldn't have left you. They didn't even call while you were in the hospital."

I looked to Mark to help me as he approached us at the picnic table, because it was too painful to contemplate that this man who disliked me so much could tell me something I didn't want to admit. My parents had left me at a time when I needed them the most. The realization that Jack was right about them and was thrusting that in my face gave me a sense of helplessness to resist the idea. Mark sat down at the picnic table and did not intercede between his father and me. I expected him to defend me from his father's observation.

"Jack, I'm concerned about you. I'll go to the emergency room with you, so you can get some help," I offered.

"Yes, Dad, let's get in the car and go to the ER," Mark said with enthusiasm. In my mind, I believed that Mark was actually seeing his father's suicidal thoughts like I was. Jack played along and the three of us went and got into Mark's car.

We drove to a different hospital this time, while Dorothy stayed with Patrick at her home. As we walked in, I saw Jack falling back behind us, and I realized that I was being prepared to go to another psychiatric unit, but this time I was angry instead of being afraid. My parents did leave me behind, and it was hard to hear about it from someone that I knew had no concern for my welfare. I was angry with Jack, my parents, and my husband, and pretty much the whole world, except for Patrick.

Irritability is a symptom of mania. I rolled up onto another locked psychiatric unit in a wheelchair, and I demanded no contact from my parents, who I decided were to blame for all of this. It was not logical, but a new experience with psychosis had begun as the anti-depressant had launched me back up into a full manic state. The fog had rolled in, and I was lost in it.

CHAPTER EIGHTEEN

PRISONER

The first day on the locked psychiatric unit, at the second medical center, started with me wandering into a large room across from my patient room. The walls were painted in muted green tones. An oblong wooden table, with five wooden chairs around it, sat just inside the doorway. Across the linoleum floor were scattered upholstered chairs and a small brown leather couch. As I walked in, I noted a nurse's station with one window open for staff to use to communicate with the patients. I was dressed in a crumpled hospital gown and pajama bottoms and slipper socks. There were about four other patients scattered in various chairs and on the couch.

A person walked toward me in this room, which was called the TV room. The person had short dishwater-blonde hair with a rounded face and body. This individual wore a shirt tucked into slacks with black loafers. I couldn't discern any facial hair. I was not sure if this person was male or female. Reality was unclear. This makes for an awkward interaction, because you don't know what pronoun to use to address them. 'The person' was holding a cup of pills, and it was meant for me. What was I going to do? I was on the couch and there were two armchairs nearby, so I kept moving towards them in hopes this person would lose interest. Finally, the person, who I took to be a nurse, managed to reach me, and I surrendered to the pursuit. "Take the pills Diana," I said to myself, "and maybe this nurse will leave you alone."

I relented and took the cup of pills and the cup of water that was offered and the nurse retreated. I sat down in the chair facing the TV up on the wall. Could they hear me through the television set? I had better be careful. I will look happy and calm and then I will be alright. I was certain they could read my mind, but I would not let them plant thoughts there. Soon, I felt the stiffness increasing in my face and hands from Haldol and the thirst that always came with lithium. The thoughts racing through my mind slowed slightly.

Mark, my husband, came through the same wooden doors that I had passed through hours earlier. He brought me clothes, which the nurses checked for anything I could use to hurt myself. I was still angry with him for what I felt was betrayal, when he had not stood up to his dad for me, and then tricked me into coming here. I demanded cigarettes from him. I had smoked half a cigarette on a dare when I was a kid, but nothing since that time. I had been raised not to smoke by my mother although my father smoked like a cracked stove, but now I didn't care what anyone thought, including Mom. My parents had driven away and left me in the deep ravine of madness to take a vacation. I specifically asked for Virginia slims. They were small, slender brown cigarettes, which I thought were sophisticated. Mark knew that this was not a battle that he was going to win, so later, the nurses delivered my first pack of cigarettes and I lit one up while I sat at a table near the nurse's station. The smoke was hot and it made my throat feel dry and I gave a small cough, but continued to puff. I flicked the ashes into an ash tray on the table, my eyes watered slightly, but I felt strong and in control.

Two young men sat on the couch, which was opposite the table, and they tried to play cards together. They were about twenty years old, one a brunette and one a blond. They were thin and nearly six foot. They seemed to know one another. Both of them were laughing and seemed perfectly content to be here. This psychiatric unit was smaller than the one I had been in at the first hospital. There was nowhere to be besides the TV room and my patient room. After I finished my cigarette I drifted back into my room.

My roommate sat on her bed. She was quiet, but one look told me to give her a wide berth. Her eyes narrowed and she glared at me, while the muscles in her face became hard and her lips were drawn straight and tight, like a coiled snake ready to strike. I had seen angry people before, but she was beyond angry. Her countenance frightened me, because there was hate in her eyes and no evidence of concern for me. That woman could smother me in my sleep, I thought. As I retreated toward the door, my roommate did not relax one muscle. Distance and nursing staff protection was my only option. I retreated back to the TV room.

Soon, the locked wooden doors that separated the locked unit from the voluntary unit were opened by another nurse and in came a man in a wheelchair. He looked around the unit quickly, leaning as far forward as he could, with a sense of amazement. He had a restraint around his waist and some on his wrists. He allowed the staff to roll him to his room. I wondered what had he done to be treated like that.

As time passed, I continued to watch the he/she person at the nurse's station, and kept my distance. I smoked periodically, which seemed like a rebellion against everyone I thought had let me down. My throat was feeling raw and sore from the smoke, but I was not ready to give up. As the night rolled on nothing seemed to happen in relation to the television as far as my thoughts were concerned. I had managed to keep thoughts from being planted in my mind.

"It's time for bed, everyone. The TV room is closed. Line up for your medication," one of the evening shift nurses instructed. When I reached the window to the nurse's station, I was handed a cup of multicolored and multi-shaped pills. I didn't recognize them.

"Tell me what you are giving me, and why," I demanded.

"This is Haldol, this is lithium, and that is Valium. They are for your manic-depression," she replied. I took the cup as instructed and took them right down. When I entered my room again, I felt a shiver go up my spine. I would try to go to sleep, hoping my roommate would not do anything to me in my sleep. I began to feel very drowsy.

An hour passed, and the room was dark, but my mind was spinning scenarios where I would die in my sleep at the hands of my roommate. Part of me wanted to fall asleep and part was too afraid to. Eventually, I walked out into the hallway and across to the TV room where I tried to lie down on the couch.

"You can't sleep in here. The TV room is closed. Go back to your room," a night shift nurse explained.

"I can't sleep."

"Go back to your room, and try again."

I felt trapped, but I didn't know what that nurse might do to me. I returned to my bed and starred at the ceiling and listened for any movement. Sometime during the night, I fell asleep.

The next morning, the man that had been in the wheelchair the day before was sitting in the TV room.

"Hey, my name is Doc Easy. I have a one-man band," he chimed in my direction as I entered the TV room.

"Hey, I'm Diana. What instruments do you play?"

"I play the harmonica, and the cymbals are on my knees, and I strum a guitar."

I felt more comfortable with him than anyone else that I had met so far. He was full of energy and talked incessantly while he puffed on a cigarette at the table. We chatted with one another, smoked, and ignored the other patients and the nursing staff.

Later that morning, the locked doors opened again, and in walked two men. I recognized one of them as Jim, who was a nurse anesthetist. Jim had graduated with me 3 years earlier. He was dressed in surgical scrubs. He saw me at nearly the same time that I noticed him, and looked shocked. He kept his distance. I felt humiliated that Jim had found me here, as a patient. Jim avoided my gaze and went on into the nursing station and began to put together equipment on a metal cart. The other man was Hispanic, and wore a suit, and I took him to be a doctor from his bearing around the nurses. It was then that I realized that neither one of the young men I had met the day before was anywhere to be seen.

As the cart rolled back out into the hall towed by Jim, I recognized the machine on the cart as one that is used in electroshock therapy. Some form of general anesthesia would be used. I concluded that this was for the two young men. The door to their room opened and Jim rolled the cart inside and closed the door behind him. In a short time Jim, along with his cart, and the doctor came out of Gary and John's room. The doctor signed a chart in the nurse's station and Jim put away the equipment and they both took their leave.

Lunch was over, and the two young men, Gary and John, still were not out of their rooms. I watched the situation with great interest. Around 5pm, Gary and John walked out of their room with their hair askew with dried gel on their temples, and continued into the TV room. They were given their dinner trays and sat silently nibbling for a short time, and then slid over to the couch. Gary picked up his guitar and plucked the strings, and then stopped and threw the guitar down on the couch. He sat with tears in his eyes.

"I can't remember," Gary said to himself. I felt sad for him. There was no laughing from either of them that evening. Electroshock can affect memory. The thought occurred that they could do the same thing to me.

That night, after the TV room was closed, I faced the same dilemma. My roommate never left our room, which is why I spent as much time in the TV room as I could, but now, again, I had to face her. She sat with her back to the corner and glared at me as I entered, much as an animal hiding in the dark with their eyes aglow. A sense of imminent harm rested throughout the entire room. I did not try to engage her in conversation, because I knew well enough not to hit a hornets' nest. Much as I had done as a child, I made myself as small as I could and I backed out of the room. Again, I tried for the TV room, and again I was sent back to my room. My stomach churned from anxiety. There would be little sleep again tonight.

Monday through Friday that week, Gary and John would repeat their electroshock treatments, and every afternoon they would walk out to the TV room. Each day they talked less until they didn't interact with others at all. Gary would try to play his guitar and John would try to play cards. Their attempts would eventually wane and they would leave and go to their rooms. I could not understand what diagnosis they could have had that made this therapeutic for them. They didn't seem better for having electroshock, but I really wasn't in my best professional frame of mind.

I had gotten over worrying about the TV reading my mind, but I still didn't know what to do with the genderless nurse. The nurse was understanding and always approached me slowly and gave me the space I needed. I complied with the medications that I was given but I had to cross-examine the medication nurse each time, because as a nurse, I knew what they should do each time they gave medication. Every morning at the crack of dawn, the lab would come and draw lithium blood levels. Out of the fog of sleep, there was a tap on my shoulder and the sharp pain of a needle in my arm. Lithium was a salt, but if the blood level was not within certain parameters, it could cause permanent damage to my kidneys. There really wasn't any other medication for manic-depression other than lithium and anti-psychotics. I was lucky to have lithium since the FDA had only made it available a few years before I came to need it. Anti-psychotics had many more side effects than lithium and so they only used them for the short term, if at all possible.

At the start of the second week of my stay, a young woman came into the unit through the locked doors. She was in a light yellow dress and a beige raincoat. She walked up to Doc Easy and sat down with him at the dining table close to the nurse's station, and tried to talk to him, but he was too easily distracted. Doc Easy was beating the table with two coffee stirrers as the staff watched him closely. The young woman was his wife. A nurse brought over a board game played with marbles and the woman and the nurse were able to divert his attention towards it. Doc and his wife were finally able to relate to each other. I invited myself to the game, which wasn't familiar to me, but I pretended to know so I could be close to Doc Easy. Sherry, Doc's wife, was pleasant and accommodating in spite of my lack of boundaries. We took turns rolling dice and moving marbles, but I really had no understanding of the game, so Sherry would help me move mine. Doc's marble would come up close to mine, and in my mind, it was a sexual advancement. I would giggle when it happened, which neither Doc nor his wife seemed to understand.

Risk-taking behaviors are common with manic persons like me. They drive too fast, have sexual trysts they normally wouldn't have, play with guns, or race trains for example. My mania was not resolving as quickly as it had done before. I was less paranoid about the nurse and the television and I wasn't talking incessantly, but there was still risky behavior born out of a delusion about Doc and myself.

Mark was allowed to see me 15 minutes a day. It seemed like he would just get there, and then he would be gone. Time passed at a snail's pace and seemed to go on forever. I could not read because of visual side effects and writing was difficult due to tremors and stiffness. There were very few activities to occupy my mind when Mark wasn't there. Longing took its toll. I found myself watching the clock much of the time.

Every morning, I would be led into a small conference room, which was attached to the nurse's station, where I would sit while the psychiatrist reviewed the nurse's notes. Each morning I would plead to see my son, Patrick. Days had gone by and no visitation from Patrick was forthcoming.

Along with the sense of loss of my family, I began to have feelings of extreme guilt. I felt as though the phone calls and visits I had made when I was first manic, especially with the religious overtones, might prevent people from following God. I pleaded to see a chaplain or a minister, but I was refused repeatedly. I felt the need to be forgiven by someone representing God.

On Tuesday morning of my third week on the unit, the doors swung open, and in walked a tall slender walnut-colored young woman with smooth skin, shining black hair, and dark brown eyes. Her beauty was striking. Her facial expression was sullen and she plopped down in one of the chairs in the TV room as soon as she entered. She smiled at Gary and John, but they didn't react as she wanted and so she went to her room in a huff.

A few minutes later, Doc Easy asked the nurses if the patients could listen to some music on the radio. The nurses turned it on and Doc asked me to dance. I jumped at the chance. I was still attracted to him, but I was able to curb my behavior better than I had done during the marble game. Neither one of us were any good at dancing, but at the time, it felt like we were.

That afternoon, Mark came for his visit. I was suddenly overcome with guilt for my delusional relationship with "Doc". I had danced with another man and played some kind of sex game. I didn't understand it myself. I just knew that Mark would leave me for good. I embraced him, and didn't want to let him go, for fear he would never come back.

"I'm sorry. I am so sorry," I said over and over. He held me and reassured me that I didn't need to apologize. Did he know what I had done? As soon as he left, I requested paper and a pencil. I wrote him an apology and begged the nurses to give it to him when he returned. I gave up the cigarettes as soon as the note was finished. I wanted his forgiveness more than anything. Mania is destructive to relationships and lives, and the guilt over all my behavior since this illness had begun bored into me like a drill.

At the end of week three, the locked doors opened and in walked Dr. D. I had worked with him in the coronary care unit in this very hospital. He stood 6 foot 6 inches tall and had very wide shoulders. He was imposing in size, and in temperament. I had seen him grab the wires belonging to a 12 lead EKG machine which were attached to a patient with suction cups across her chest, and pull them all off, leaving her covered with hickies, because he didn't like the way they were placed.

Dr. D. would show up for rounds with a large "iced tea", which was more than tea. The unbelievable part of it all was that he really was a good cardiologist, but he hated it, and his temper frightened everyone. Now, he was standing over his walnut-colored daughter in a locked psychiatric unit, where neither his daughter nor I could escape. He sat down next to his daughter, and ignored me, which suited me just fine. Eventually, he left, but I knew he would be back. I breathed a sigh of relief when he was gone, but now there was a new sense of distress.

Mark came to visit me a short time after Dr. D. left. I was pacing up and down the hallway and talking to myself.

I ran from the hall into the TV room, and yelled, "I am signing out AMA right now!" using the acronym for 'against medical advice'. "Mark, get me out of here!" I pleaded.

Mark walked over to me and gently laid his hands on my shoulders to try to calm me down. The nurses scrambled from the nurse's station.

"Diana, you need to settle down, right now," one of the nurses told me firmly.

I suddenly realized that this was no idle threat. I wasn't there as a voluntary patient, and the nurses could do whatever they wanted to do to me. I was a prisoner. The feelings of betrayal surged again. I sat down hard into a chair by the table and let that thought soak in. How would I get out of here? I was without any power in this situation. There would be an increase in my medication that afternoon I was sure, since I had made a loud scene. The nurse asked Mark to leave, and loneliness and vulnerability struck me like a tidal wave.

The evening that followed my realization of being an involuntary patient was quiet and I was too. I had shut down and did not even make eye contact. The consequences for a wrong action might mean even more time here. I would tread lightly. Out of nowhere, there was screaming and I heard glass breaking and tinkling as it hit the linoleum. Up the hall Dr. D.'s daughter came running with blood flying everywhere. She had broken the glass over the fire extinguisher and cut herself. The locked doors began to buzz and in came several men, one after another, and they picked her up and dragged her kicking and screaming to her room at the end of the hall. One of the nurses walked down the hall with a syringe of medication and leather restraints, while Dr. D.'s daughter continued to yell and curse and bang against the side rails of her bed. Eventually, she got quiet, and in came a doctor in his surgical scrubs to stitch her up. The next morning, she was discharged from the unit. Is that what you had to do to get out of here? Did you act out and then you would get out?

While Dr. D.'s daughter transferred out of the unit, my nurse for the day asked me to go to my room. For once, my roommate wasn't there. The nurse sat down on a chair while I sat on my bed.

"Diana, you need to learn how to talk to your doctor."

"Learn how to talk to the doctor? What do you mean? I thought that I did talk to him."

"Diana, you need to let him know how you are doing."

"Okay," I said, feeling confused

This made no sense to me. I had talked to doctors for years. I thought I had told him how I was. Soon thereafter, my nurse took me to the small conference room to see my doctor. He sat in his usual chair and studied the nurse's notes without looking up as I entered the claustrophobic room.

"I think I'm doing better," I volunteered.

He made no reply at first, and then nodded in acknowledgement.

"I'll see you tomorrow." This was the shortest meeting we had had since I arrived.

"Can I please see my son?" I asked again, as I had been doing for what seemed like forever.

"You can see him today," he said without any exchange of glances. My nurse proceeded to call Mark to make arrangements. That afternoon, my roommate was discharged from the hospital. Things were looking up.

In the early evening, as the air cooled, I was allowed to leave the unit with Mark. Down three floors by elevator, my excitement increased with each ding for the floors. I strode with Mark to the front lobby of the hospital, where Mark's mom, Dorothy, sat holding Patrick, my son. Pat was growing so fast. He sat on her lap in a little light blue sweatsuit with a hood. His hair was such a light blonde that you could hardly tell he had any, but he was starting to get little ringlets. Dorothy handed him to me and I looked into his little blue eyes. There wasn't really the sign of recognition there that I remembered and he turned to look back at Dorothy. I talked to him and he turned back to look at my face. I knew that if I just had more time with him, we would bond again.

Outside the hospital, you could hear the high pitch of sirens coming toward the front of the building. I wasn't paying much attention to them, until an employee walked up to us and told us to stay where we were.

"What's going on out there? Mark asked.

"A patient that was discharged from the psychiatric unit came back here to shoot her doctor," the employee explained. I knew that it must have been my discharged roommate who had gone home and gotten a gun and had come back to try to shoot her doctor. This didn't surprise me, and I was relieved that she wouldn't be coming back to my room. I knew for sure then that I had to get home somehow. Instead, after a brief 15 minutes, I had to hand Patrick back to Dorothy. My arms ached.

When Mark left me at the doors with the nurses, I decided to take a shower. No one could see me cry in the shower. How did cutting yourself with broken glass get you out of here? It wasn't fair. I had behaved myself, and yet here I was. I began to pound my fists against the slippery tiles of the hot shower. I was not the type to cut myself. I was stuck in this psychiatric unit and my hope lagged. I was a prisoner here, but I hadn't done anything that I should be locked up for. I began to pray.

"God, they won't let me talk to a minister or anyone in the priesthood. You will have to minister to me. I want your forgiveness and I want to go home."

The third week began to wind down, when I found myself again in the conference room with the psychiatrist.

"Diana, I want you to remember that you are not a nurse while you are here. You are a patient, okay?"

"Yes, sir."

I wasn't sure what I had done to have that stressed to me. I decided I would dance to his tune, because he held my freedom in his hands.

Lunchtime came and went. Most of the patients were seated around the TV room. I heard the buzz for the doors again, and saw them open. In came a woman about my mother's age that was having trouble walking. My first impulse was to jump up and help her, but I didn't out of fear of what my psychiatrist would think. The woman struggled to the first chair she could get to. The guilt of just sitting there made me feel bad and angry, but I was afraid of losing the opportunity to go home. A few steps behind her was Edward, an elder in my church's priesthood, with her suitcase in his hands.

In that moment I heard in my mind: "There is no place you can be that I cannot be with you."

God had gotten a minister through those doors unbeknownst to the nursing staff. It reassured me that I was not alone in this place. God was with me.

That evening, my nurse came to get me.

"Diana, your mom wants to talk to you. Is that alright?"

"Sure," I said, rather stunned. I had forgotten that I had not wanted to talk with my parents when I arrived.

"Mom?" I said into the receiver.

"Diana, I have been trying to talk to you for days. I kept calling, but they wouldn't confirm you were even there. Mark had told us you were there, so finally I just told them that I would go to the administrator if they didn't let me talk to you," she said. "How are you?"

"I'm alright, I guess."

"I have been so worried about you, honey."

"Thanks Mom."

"Hey, Sis, this is Dad. Do you remember me? Can you remember how to be a nurse?"

"Yes, sure." I wondered if he thought being mentally ill meant you couldn't do what you used to do. It perturbed me.

"Good," He said with a small sigh. It felt like decades since I had worked, but I had not forgotten anything. The nursing staff cut the call short, and I said good-bye. At least my parents had been interested enough to call, I thought. It would be a long time before I could forgive them for leaving me when I was so ill and going on their vacation instead.

After being in this place that felt more like a jail than a hospital for almost a month, I began to feel this inner physical uneasiness. I wasn't sure what that meant, but I had trouble sitting still. There was a swivel chair in the TV room, and I would sit and swivel back and forth, and back and forth, and then I would get up and pace in the hallway up and down, and up and down. From one to the other I would go almost continually. The nursing staff didn't seem to notice much, and I figured that it must have to do with being here as long as I had been. Doc Easy had been discharged, as well as Gary and John. Gary and John had completed 15 ECT treatments over the first 3 weeks I had been there. I didn't have a roommate at this point, but even at that, I found that it was hard to rest quietly. When I finally said something to one of the staff about it, they decided that I must have some pent-up anger that I needed to get rid of. They gave me a Nerf bat and had me beat the couch. It didn't help.

By the middle of the fourth week I was very tired from perpetual motion, but I couldn't stop. The restless feeling was only relieved with constant motion. As I walked down the hallway on my millionth trip, one of the evening nurses watched me.

"Diana, come back here for a minute." I walked back towards her.

"Now, walk away from me."

I complied. I had become so stiff from the antipsychotic medication, Haldol, that I wasn't even swinging my arms as I walked anymore. She had me come and sit down. While I sat, she had me put my elbow on the table and then moved my right forearm up and down, and it jerked haltingly like the sprockets on a gear. I didn't know it then, but it was a side effect called cog wheeling. The restlessness turned out to be a side effect of antipsychotics called akathisia. She called the doctor, and he reduced the Haldol dose, and put me on Cogentin for the side effects. What a relief to be freed from that hell.

Out of the blue, two days later, my doctor said that I could go on pass, with some other patients, to a movie. We walked together to the elevator and down to the main floor, and then out the front door, led by and followed by staff. I felt conspicuous because we were obviously being guarded, but the sun was bright, and the air smelled tantalizing. I had not had fresh air for over a month. We walked down the block and climbed into a beige van with a hospital logo. We entered the theatre in the same fashion that we had walked to the van. We saw "Blue Velvet", which was a remake of the original. It wasn't particularly good, but it was away from what I had come to know as confinement.

At the end of September, I received a letter from my mother. She had called me every few nights. The letter covered basic news but then there were these words:

"Honey, I don't have much of anything but work. I just wish I could be there and take you in my arms and kiss your problems away like I did when you were small, if it would work. I'd sure try it."

I teared up as I read it. I just wished she had stayed in Wichita when she saw how sick I was in the first place. I knew she was sincere in her letter and so I took the comfort that was offered.

Weeks 5 and 6 seemed to run together. Every day they would let me go with a group of patients out on a roof where we could play volleyball, or just sit and enjoy the sun and fresh air. Slowly, they reduced the Haldol, until I wasn't getting it any longer, and that made me feel freer, as the stiffness, visual changes, and constipation went away.

The lithium continued, as did the daily blood tests, until one morning a lab person came in and all of a sudden, it was too much. I was tired of being poked every morning for weeks, and I hated being controlled and being afraid. I refused to let her draw the blood, and kept my bed between the two of us. This was the only control I had left. I didn't threaten her, but I was emphatic. An hour later, a nun in her white habit, who was head of the lab, came in and talked me into letting her draw the lithium blood level yet again. She informed me that the order would be changed to once a week. It was a small victory, but at least I had that.

Towards week six, I was moved to the open unit. I had started feeling sadder each day and had difficulty getting myself up and around. I was ruminating like a cow chewing its cud over and over. I had always been a confident person and had never had trouble in school or with whatever I set my mind on. Eventually I would meet my goals. Now, that part of me was gone. The continual reflection on all that had happened to me pounded my confidence into the ground. I wasn't sure I could do anything that I had done before, including caring for Patrick. This experience had become a line of demarcation separating BC from AD in my life.

On the last day of week six, Mark was invited to meet with my psychiatrist when he made rounds on me. My doctor was discharging me.

"Mrs. Dodds, I am discharging you today. We have set up outpatient follow-up for you. I will not be continuing with your care outside of the hospital." He informed me.

I felt a spike in fear. This doctor had made me so dependent on him for everything in my life for six weeks, and now all of a sudden he was walking away. How would I be able to manage? Without much time to contemplate this change, I was packed up, and out the front hospital doors I walked with Mark. Out in the parking lot, I began to cry uncontrollably. A car stopped as it was coming out of the doctor's portion of the lot. My psychiatrist was behind the wheel.

"Is everything alright? Do you need some help?"

"No, we'll be alright," Mark replied.

I knew right there and then, that it was not alright. I was lost and afraid. How would I ever face my life again?

ECT Definition

By Mayo Clinic Staff

Electroconvulsive therapy (ECT) is a procedure, done under general anesthesia, in which small electric currents are passed through the brain, intentionally triggering a brief seizure. ECT seems to cause changes in brain chemistry that can quickly reverse symptoms of certain mental illnesses.

ECT often works when other treatments are unsuccessful and when the full course of treatment is completed, but it may not work for everyone.

Much of the stigma attached to ECT is based on early treatments in which high doses of electricity were administered without anesthesia, leading to memory loss, fractured bones and other serious side effects.

ECT is much safer today. Although ECT still causes some side effects, it now uses electric currents given in a controlled setting to achieve the most benefit with the fewest possible risks.

Source: http://www.mayoclinic.org/tests-procedures/electroconvulsive-therapy/basics/definition/prc-20014161

CHAPTER NINETEEN

REVELATIONS

It is amazing how humble you can become so that you can see your child again. Each day, after coming home from my last psychiatric admission, I would sit in the recliner in my in-laws' home and be as quiet and calm as I could possibly be. In the living room in the large, classic black English carriage, Patrick lay napping. In the room, also, was a baby sitter who watched Patrick and me all day. I had to ask permission to hold him, or anything else I wished to do with him. When you love your child, you swallow your pride because you hope and pray that one day he will be yours completely again.

At night, I would go home alone, and leave Patrick behind. Each time, my heart would be broken again, and a deep loneliness would take hold. There was no time limit set for this arrangement, and so I would summon strength to go back each day. After nearly a month of this routine, I implored Jack and Dorothy, my in-laws, to let Mark and I take him home for a couple of hours.

I was overjoyed when Mark walked in the front door of our small white rental house with Pat. I held Patrick, talked to him, rocked him, and fed him and I felt as close to normal as I had felt for months. After two hours, Mark was preparing to take him back to his parent's house, and Patrick began to cry. Mark began to panic and got a cool, wet washrag to try to keep Patrick's face from turning red. He feared what his parents might think. That was the end of my patience and humility.

"He is not going back," I said.

"He has to," Mark replied.

"No, he doesn't. He is our son." And so it was settled. Patrick was finally home with us both.

After a week living back home with us again, I asked Mark to help me take Patrick to Goodland to see my parents. It was a six-hour ride from Wichita, but I was happy to be out of town and away from the events that I had just lived through. Upon arriving at my parents' home, as I walked up to the porch, a blue and white 56 Chevy pulled up in front. Out of the car came my aunt Marie. She worked at the hospital in town, and she had heard that I was home for a visit. Walking up to me, she wrapped her arms around me and said,

"Finally, somebody understands."

What an odd thing to say. I accepted her hug, but had no idea what she could mean by her statement. Later, that evening, after Marie had headed for home, I began to quiz my mom about what Marie had meant.

"Mom, what did Marie mean about me understanding? What do I understand?"

"Well, when Marie was a teenager, Grandma Middleton had to take her to California for electric shock treatments," Mom replied in a matter-of-fact way.

"What? You never told me that before!"

"Oh, I guess I never thought much about it."

I was flabbergasted that my family had kept such a secret. The fact that the family often made fun of her began to make sense. That must have been so frightening for her at such a young age. They did not use muscle-paralyzing drugs in those days and so the seizure that she would have had after each electric treatment would have caused a joint-wrenching reaction.

I confronted my dad about this revelation later that night.

"Is that why you kept asking me if I remembered how to be a nurse?" I queried.

"Yea, she had to repeat a whole year of school when she came back, because she couldn't remember a lot of things." Pieces began to fall into place. As the discussion continued, I learned that Grandpa Middleton had become so depressed during the dirty thirties that he was going to sell the whole farm for a popcorn machine that sat on the corner in town. That seemed like an understandable response to those times, but Grandma didn't think so. She refused to let him do it. There was also Uncle Watts, as he was called. His actual name was David. He was my father's great uncle and all that Dad had ever heard about him was that he was peculiar, whatever that meant.

I began to realize the secrets that my family had kept had left me on a cliff about to fall, and I had never realized it. There was one epiphany after another as I began to put my father's behavior over the years into a new perspective. When you grow up with someone as unpredictable and moody as he was, you think that it's normal, but it wasn't. No one in my immediate family seemed to realize that my father was also ill. I would ponder these revelations for years and when mental illness began cropping up elsewhere in the family, it all made complete sense.

CHAPTER TWENTY

THE VALLEY OF THE SHADOW

Upon our return from a trip to Goodland in November of 1978, Mark, my son Patrick, and I began trying to recapture what is often called "a normal life", or as normal as a life can be after a mental unit admission. As a nurse, Mark had to get back to his full-time job as a staff RN on a medical/surgical unit that was a step-down unit from intensive care. He was a recently graduated RN, but was already sought after on his unit. He had come so far from the shy stuttering man that I had married and so much had been foisted onto his shoulders over these months of my first manic event.

For Patrick and I, it was back to being a mother and her son. Patrick was becoming reacquainted with me and he smiled when I held him. He had grown so much. When I went to the hospital, he was only 2 months old, but now he was 5 going on six months old. He was curious and was using his seated walker to go everywhere. There was a tray that surrounded him and four castors that allowed him to move around. Mark and his parents had put him in the walker as soon as his feet could hit the floor, and he immediately began to mobilize himself. Now, he would start running in one direction, plant his feet, grab the tray of the walker and change the direction and take off on that tangent. He remained a little toe-head, with very light blonde hair that was beginning to form ringlets, and bright blue eyes that saw everything and wanted to know about everything, including putting everything in his mouth. Mealtimes were as much play as nutrition. This led to the yellow tubby and a bath. He smelled so good when he was done, and I cuddled him as I dried him off and put on his diaper. For such an energetic guy, these were special times.

With each passing day, I noticed sadness creeping into my thoughts. An active infant kept my mind occupied when he was awake, but when he finally gave into a nap, my mind filled with thoughts of hopelessness. Each day, when I arose to fix breakfast and change Patrick, the same melancholy began imposing itself like a troublesome visitor that wouldn't leave. After two weeks of these intrusions, the hopelessness turned palpable and unrelenting. Thoughts of harming myself began nibbling at the frayed edges of my reflections. I pushed the feelings out over and over. Take an overdose of those medications. Slit your wrists. Walk out in front of a car.

The cold hands of depression not only gripped my mind, but began to take control of my body as well. I felt my energy waning. Each activity meant that I had to push myself. To get out of bed was an achievement. Doing any kind of daily hygiene seemed too momentous to undertake. In spite of this, Patrick was fed, bathed, diapers changed, and as it was being done, I mentally begged him to sleep. What does a mother who feels like this look like to an infant?

Every moment became a wound upon my spirit. It became painful to be awake. Sleep is the only pain relief for feelings such as these. When you have an infant to care for, you wear those wounds even though every fiber of your being cries for escape, because you have your son home, and you do not dare relinquish that responsibility again or you may never get him back. There would be no antidepressants to help with this mood. The risk of being pushed up into mania was too great.

When I had been discharged from the psychiatric unit in October, it was with a plan for outpatient follow-up. The public mental health department was following my progress. I was to meet my counsellor at the county mental health center. It was a one-story cement block building painted in a pale grey-blue, and set back from the main streets. There was a small sign on the side of the building. Unconsciously, I glanced in the rearview mirror to see if anyone could see me turning into the parking lot. No one was behind me. I chastised myself for being so self-conscious. I walked from my parked car across the crushed stone drive and through the glass doors. The office was divided from a very small waiting area by a large opening where a half wall with a ledge and sliding glass window divided the patients from the office staff. I walked up to the windowsill.

"Hello, my name is Diana Dodds. I have an appointment with Susan."

"Have a seat over there, and we will be with you in just a moment."

I felt reluctant at the thought and stood there before catching myself and looking around for a seat. I sat myself in a chair isolated from my neighbor by an empty one. I hoped that no one that I knew would walk by and see me. As a student nurse, I had spent time at a center similar to this and I hoped no students would be in today. A sense of shame swept over me. I thought of Aunt Marie's experience with electrical shock treatment and my dad's family's reaction to it, and I finally understood why she had kept her secret. I glanced at the other people sitting in chairs waiting for their appointments and it felt as though there was a large "M" on my forehead. Society was not kind to the mentally ill, because it was seen as a character flaw or a weakness. Even in nursing school, they blamed it on how you were raised. I noticed that no one in the room looked at anyone else, and I realized that there was an unspoken agreement, among all of us sitting there, to remain anonymous.

"Diana, could you follow me?" a young stocky woman said to me. I noticed immediately that she did not look at me, but in my general direction. I followed her down the short hallway to the office at the end. She walked stiffly and deliberately.

"Have a seat. My name is Susan. I will be your counsellor."

As I sat myself down, I noticed that Susan's eyes moved around constantly, and did not focus on anything. It occurred to me that she was visually impaired.

"How have you been doing since you got home from the hospital?"

"Well, not so good," I said, searching for some way to explain what I had been feeling.

"When you say, 'not so good', could you give me some examples?"

"I've been taking care of my son, but I'm having trouble getting everything done."

"What kind of things have you been able to do?"

"Not much."

"Just give me some examples, Diana."

"Oh, you know. Changing diapers, making up food and feeding my son, giving him a bath."

"It sounds to me that you think you should be doing more," Susan stated.

"Yes," I said as tears began to form and my throat ached.

"I think you are struggling. Are you feeling down?"

"Yes," I said, as though the emotional dam might break at any moment.

"Are you having suicidal thoughts?"

There was a frightening moment when I realized that admitting to suicidal thoughts might mean losing my son, but I didn't want to lose this battle with life and death.

"Yes, I have... but I won't do anything."

"I'm glad to hear that. There is something I want you to do. I want you to write down everything you do all day and bring it with you the next time you come."

"Alright," I said with nearly a question in my voice. I took a chance and waved my hand in front of her. No response. Susan was blind! How could she pick up on my emotional state so well without being able to see my demeanor? She was obviously skilled at picking up emotional state from voice alone.

"Promise me that if you begin to feel like you might harm yourself, that you will call the emergency number."

"I will."

"Good. It is hard right now, but we will work to make things better. I'm glad to meet you. I will see you in three days. Please stop at the desk and make an appointment." She stood and showed me to her office door and closed it behind me. My hope for survival in this situation rested in the hands of a blind woman.

The next time I saw Susan, she had me read the list of what I had done every day, and she suggested that as bad as I was feeling, and how difficult it was to summon both the physical and emotional energy to do anything, that I was doing well. Never in my life had just getting out of bed seemed like an achievement that I should feel proud of. This small exercise that Susan had me do helped to keep me from the guilt that so often goes with depression. That guilt can magnify the pain.

This was the downside after mania, and I knew it, and I prayed for my mood to swing back up to normal. Until my mood made that swing, I longed each day for Patrick to nap. That nap was like rain on arid land. As soon as his eyelids fluttered closed, I would go downstairs to the basement where we had a guest bed. I would lie across that bed and thoughts would go round and round in my head about ways and means to kill myself. To fight these torrents that threatened to take me to my next life, I would put on a record with one particular song that talked about reasons to live. The song spoke about a worker and a lover and a mother and her son and I played it over and over and over. When I would hear about the mother and her son, I would think how terrible it would be for my husband to find me if I did commit suicide and I thought about Patrick hating me for leaving him.

This was like being out on the open ocean, treading water to keep your head up, to keep air coming into your lungs. How long can you keep up the fight before the body and mind give in to the inevitable and you sink beneath the waves? The words of the song were like an argument that I was having with myself. As it played, I would sing out that I wanted to live as if to convince myself. Eventually, I would hear Patrick crying upstairs, and the song ended and I was back to pushing through the pain and doing the work of caring, without the feelings that should go with it.

It occurred to me that God had told me that my experience with Sophia's suicide, while in nursing school, would work for good. I could not imagine anything good coming from a friend's suicide, but I now understood that my memory of finding her had informed me about what my suicide would do to my husband. I could imagine him finding me hard and cold. I could imagine the toll it would take on him to lose me, and to be left to parent Patrick alone. The emotional toll on Mark would be beyond measure. God had taken a terrible experience and used it to save me, and them. That experience made me fight harder. The song on the record, and my memories of Sophia, became a life preserver, while I fought the waves of this sea of torment.

At one of the follow-up visits with my counsellor, Susan, we discussed stressors in my life that might be contributing to the depression I was fighting. One of those stressors was conversations with my father-in-law.

"Diana, can you give me an example of things that your father-in-law might say?" Susan inquired.

"It usually has to do with Mark. He would ask me if I thought Mark could be a doctor. He doesn't like the fact that Mark is just a nurse."

"Alright, you pretend to be your father-in-law, and I will pretend to be you. What would he say?"

"Diana, don't you think Mark would be better off if he were a doctor?"

"It could be," she replied

"Well, you think he can do it, don't you?" I said in my best Jack tone.

"Possible," Susan said, unfazed. "Do you see how you're answering the question, but he is not sure of your answer?"

"Yes."

"That is called fogging."

Fogging kept Jack off balance and gave me relief from his ongoing pressure. These techniques were coping skills that returned some power back to me to help myself.

Besides the daily emotional toll of the depression, there were the physical effects of the lithium I was taking. There was a constant thirst, and the equally constant need to urinate. Lithium causes fine tremor in the hands. To work as a nurse required a steady hand, and I wondered if I'd ever be able to work again. My scalp began to itch and infrequent flaking turned into raging psoriasis. Lithium seemed to escalate the skin disorder. On top of those side effects was weight gain. All of the results of taking lithium became another stressor. But lithium was the only mood stabilizing agent in those days. The only other choices were the anti-psychotics and awful side effects of them, which I had already experienced in the hospital. I kept reminding myself that this was the price I paid to live in my home with my husband and son.

As the early days of December dawned, I had no desire to celebrate the holidays. The holidays underscored the despondency that had become my daily life. Cheerful sparkling lights bedecked the neighborhood, while my home sat in darkness. There was no Christmas tree. The idea of shopping for gifts and pushing through busy buyers was too overwhelming to contemplate. Without my income, Christmas in 1978 was very slim in the gift department anyway. I took an old Radio wagon from Mark's childhood, and repainted it for Patrick to ride in. It took all that I could summon to do it, but he seemed to enjoy riding in it. I spent the holiday with Mark's family. My face was like a mask set with a smile and all the energy that I could summon was used to appear cheerful. The tension among us was palpable, but when it was time to go home from my in-laws' house, no effort was made to keep Patrick with them.

With the dawn of 1979, I trudged on, but with a wisp of hope in the techniques that Susan taught me from week to week. Many of those techniques strengthened relationships. A support system is critical in keeping mood-impaired people afloat. I still withheld my suicidal thoughts from Mark, out of fear of losing Patrick, but he had become a skillful reader of my nonverbal cues and would hold me and whisper in my ear that this too would pass.

As February of 1979 commenced, I began noticing that my hair was breaking easily. My face and hands became puffy. The fatigue that I had fought since being discharged from the hospital, in October of 1978, had been increasing and I found keeping up with Patrick's care and the housekeeping of a small rental house harder and harder. My mood remained unchanged. One day when I was brushing my teeth in front of the bathroom mirror, I swallowed some water and noticed a lump in my throat. I swallowed again, and I could see my thyroid was enlarged as it moved up and down. I had a goiter! The thyroid requires iodine to make thyroid hormone. When there isn't enough iodine in the diet, the thyroid gets larger in an effort to keep thyroid hormone levels where they should be. Since iodine had been added to table salt long ago, you didn't see goiters as often.

Like the circle of life, I found myself again at Dr. H.'s office. I didn't have a family doctor, and Dr. H., my OB/GYN doctor, had become both friend and doctor. He felt the goiter right away when he examined me. Down the hall he went to talk to a hormone specialist who worked in his building. Next, he was on the phone with my psychiatrist. They all concurred that I must stop the lithium. Lithium, as a salt, was competing with table salt containing iodine, and edged out the table salt, thus the thyroid had enlarged. The goiter was approximately 4 inches wide and it was thicker than normal. He put me on a short prescription of thyroid replacement to help my thyroid to recover and shrink back to a normal size.

Now, I waited for the sky to fall. I had been taken off lithium. Would the mania return? Would I fall deeper into depression, and be pulled under the waves? As days passed and turned into weeks, the mania did not return. I began to have more, but not excessive, energy. That fine line of normal mood was being redrawn. I felt pleasure again in everyday things: my baby's laugh, my husband's smile, and being able to read a book when Patrick went down for a nap. The intrusive suicidal thoughts slowly disappeared. Keeping up with a growing child, with growing abilities to crawl and walk, was easier. His naps were just naps. The goiter disappeared. I began to have hope of being normal again, and I gave God thanks for keeping me alive through the seven months since my discharge from the psychiatric unit. I thanked him for being with me through the valley of the shadow.

CHAPTER TWENTY-ONE

CINDY

Cindy, a close friend of mine from Wesley School of Nursing, stood 5 foot tall, with short, straight, black hair and silver metal rim glasses. Cindy was a funny person and always up to something. She was forever doing something to her roommate at Wesley and they went round and round, but it was all in good fun. She always did well in school and was serious when she cared for patients.

Cindy had once gathered all my friends, to stare through the glass mailbox windows behind the desk at the dormitory, when Mark came to pick me up for a date. She knew from our conversations that he was shy, so she made sure that all those same friends met both of us in the social lounge across from the desk to draw him into our conversation and kept it light and fun. Like a social bridge, Cindy made Mark feel comfortable talking and interacting with my friends.

"Mark, these are my friends Cindy, Nancy, and Mary. Mary is my roommate."

"Hello," Mark answered.

"Hey, Mark, what do you do?" Cindy queried.

"Oh, well, I work as an orderly at St. Joseph Medical Center."

"That's a lot like what we and Diana do. What part do you like the best?"

"I really like intensive care. I've been telling Diana about what I've learned," Mark replied with a grin on his face. Cindy had opened the door and Mark stepped through.

After Mark and I became engaged, two different groups of girls threw me in the shower, which was a tradition at the dormitory. I complained that it wasn't fair that Mark hadn't shared the experience, and so my friends hatched a plan to make it up to me. On one of our gatherings in the first floor activity room, the scheme commenced.

"Hey, guys, why don't we all go out for ice cream?" Cindy suggested. Everyone chimed in affirmation of the idea.

"Oh, I forgot that I've got to have my back x-rayed before I can go up on the floor tomorrow. My doctor says it's routine." She was telling the truth about the x-ray, so it had the sound of truth to it, and Mark believed her completely.

"We'll go with you to get the x-ray," I said, sensing the plan was afoot.

As we followed her out the door, the girls rushed Mark and lifted him up off of the floor and carried him to a bathroom at the end of the hall, and in that bathroom was a shower. I allowed myself to drift back as Mark and my friends passed me, and I began to chuckle.

"It's about time!" I said triumphantly.

"Oh, really?" Cindy replied. With that comment, my friends turned and into the shower I went with Mark. It was a bonding experience for all of us.

On the following October, when Mark and I got married, Cindy was my maiden of honor. During the wedding pictures before the ceremony, Cindy posed as she helped me on with a wedding garter. The sanctuary was decorated in maroon and white flowers, with white bows on the ends of the rows of seats. Cindy and my other friend Nancy were dressed in their maroon dresses and they marched up the aisle accompanied by Mark's groomsmen in their maroon tuxedos. With the glow of candles on the rostrum, and the large stained-glass picture of Christ kneeling in the Garden of Gethsemane, Mark and I stood before Elder Burl Allen and were bonded before God.

Cindy and the rest of my friends helped decorate our car and booby-trap our bedroom as we spent our time in the wedding reception. I expected nothing less. As the next three years went by, Cindy, Mark, and I became closer friends.

When I became pregnant with Patrick, we asked Cindy if she would consider being his godmother. She was thrilled at the prospect. On the night that I went to the labor department at Wesley, Cindy waited with Mark's parents as Mark kept them abreast of progress. After the C-section that brought Patrick into the world, Mark went to announce his birth to them.

"Mom, Dad, we have a little boy. Diana had to have an emergency C-section, but Patrick is doing fine."

"Oh, Mark, that is wonderful. How is Diana?"

"She's doing fine. She's in the recovery room. We should be able to see Patrick in the nursery in a few minutes."

"I'm a godmother!" Cindy squealed, as she wrapped her arms around Mark in a tight squeeze, picked him up off the floor, and swung him around. Three weeks later, when we had Patrick's blessing at church, Cindy was there. We called her Aunt Cindy from that time forward.

Cindy, Nancy, and my roommate Mary gave us a baby shower. Mark's half-sister Susan was there along with Dorothy, Mark's mother. Patrick was passed from one to another, charming them as he went. As the gifts were opened, I wondered what Cindy had decided to give him. She excused herself from the front room of the little white house where we were living and came back through the front door with a huge English perambulator. This carriage was big enough to hold a 4-year-old child and had water-proof coverings that would allow me to walk in almost any weather.

From the time of Patrick's baby shower, until after I came home from my first two-week psychiatric hospitalization, I had not seen Cindy. I became more with-drawn and slept a good share of the time. Cindy came to see me. We both sat on the edge of my bed and she tried all the things she used to do to try to "cheer" me up. The problem with depression is that you can't shake it off just because you may want to, or when others do things to try and cheer you. Cindy left after trying everything she knew to do, and within a week, I was back in the hospital again.

After the hospitalizations for mania, and after being home again with Patrick I began to try and reconnect with my world. I called Cindy in November, and got an answering machine twice, and no phone call back. I knew that she was working full-time, so I dismissed it. At Christmas time, there was a knock at the front door, and by the time I got there, I saw Cindy's van driving away and on the porch was a gift for Patrick. I knew she loved him, and perhaps needed to be somewhere. I sent her a Christmas card with a thank you for the gift, in hopes we would reconnect. I didn't hear back from her, and then on Patrick's birthday in May of the following year, again a knock came at the door and again, Cindy drove away before I could get to the door. I wasn't sure the reason for this change, but my illness seemed to be one possibility to consider. Since the last time that Cin-dy and I had visited, she had moved and I didn't have her address, so I decided to go to her nursing unit at the hospital to ask that question. To assume that someone thinks something without knowing for sure can lead you astray. I walked onto her unit and saw her at the nurse's station.

"Cindy, I don't want to bother you, but do you have a minute to talk to me?" I asked.

"Yes, if you can meet me in the medication room."

I followed her there. "You've come to my house a couple of times and dropped off things for Patrick, but you drove away before I could get to the door, and you haven't responded to my efforts to contact you. Is there a problem that I don't know about?"

The question hung in the air for a moment and Cindy looked down at the floor to avoid my gaze and took a deep breath.

"Yes...My counsellor told me that I should stop seeing you."

"Your counsellor? Why?"

"He said that you're not a good influence in my life."

"Not a good influence? What did I do?"

" I can't be around you.."

"Oh," I said. I was stunned to silence, and retreated from the room as tears began welling up in my eyes.

This illness that I had not caused, and did not want, had caused collateral damage that I had not expected. It never occurred to me that one of my best friends, and an RN to boot, would choose to withdraw her friendship from me because of my bipolar disease. I had managed to survive my depression, but had lost a friend. As years went by, this same experience crept up more than once. The reasons for the estrangement from friends and acquaintances varied from person to person, but underlying those reasons always seemed to be a sense of fear. If Diana can become bipolar, could something like that happen to me?

Mental illness developing in someone you know and trust can shake trust in your own mental health. I would eventually make friends of those who accepted this part of me, as just a part, and not all of me. It was a learning experience, and it became obvious to me that I would make decisions about revealing my illness to perspective friends carefully and after that trust was already there. I could not pretend to be someone that I wasn't. Hiding is painful and drains the joy out of living.

CHAPTER TWENTY-TWO

RESURRECTION

After passing through the dark shadows of depression, I began to feel as though I was given another chance at life. Uncertainties and fear dogged my steps each day, and yet deep down the desire to return to nursing kept pushing against that trepidation. The idea of working in the hospital seemed out of reach. Then, my memory of a place I once observed as a student nurse popped into my mind. The Minor Surgery Center of Wichita was the second day surgery center in the United States. The owners of the Wichita Surgery Center had gone to Phoenix, Arizona, the first center, to learn a new way to provide this service. The surgery center in Wichita belonged to two anesthesiologists. As a student, I had observed this facility and how they dealt with little children who naturally are apprehensive with strangers and procedures. The center's way around that was to let the child pick a stuffed animal to hold while they were admitted and to take with them into the operating room. When they were asleep, the animal was put on their stretcher, so it was there when they woke up. I knew anyone who cared that much for their smallest clients, could be willing to give me a chance.

This was 1979, and there was no protection for people with mental illness. The secret of my psychotic break would have to be kept close to my vest. Fortunately for me, they were looking for nurses at the center. I put on my most professional-looking clothes to appear as serious as I could. I was given an application and filled it out with a sigh of relief because there were no questions there that would indicate that I had a mental health issue. Now, I waited for a verdict.

Two weeks into April of '79, a call came. Helen, the woman at the other end of the phone, was very businesslike and we made an appointment to meet. Two days after the call, I met Helen in her office. She was slender and slightly taller than me at about 5 foot 4 inches. She had brown curly hair and wore half glasses on a chain and she looked over the rims of her glasses as she reviewed my application with me. She quizzed me about the jobs that I had had and why I had left them. I convinced her that the 10 months that I had been away from work was because I had given birth to my first son. That satisfied her curiosity. Not being completely honest felt wrong. The acceptance of my partial truth now nested in my mind and fear grew out of it.

In response, that fear became a resolute conviction that I must prove that I had the right to be there. I was shown the ropes of this new job and proceeded to do each piece of it to the best of my ability. I was placed on the admission team, and then after everyone was admitted, I was sent to the recovery room. I stood next to Helen and she showed me the best way to recover both adults and children. She was a nurse anesthetist and so I gladly did whatever she recommended as she had more advanced knowledge that I could glean.

Helen and the other recovery room nurses all did exactly the same work that I did. This was a comforting feeling because the person who would determine my ongoing employment knew exactly what my job entailed. We developed a camaraderie, as we stood side by side holding people's heads to keep their airways open until they were awake enough to do it themselves.

The surgeons did oral surgery, tied women's fallopian tubes, did ear tubes, circumcisions, and vasectomies, as well as any other minor procedure that didn't require a hospital stay. We were usually done by 2pm from Monday through Thursday, and on Friday we had longer days for those patients that wanted extra days to recover. Every Friday, the owners of the center would buy lunch for everyone. After a long day caring for patients, it was like having a picnic with friends.

The first duty of each day was meeting at the ice machine to fill ice bags for the patients that required them. We would talk about our families and life events, and tell jokes to one another. One woman, Jane, was petite with brunette hair and glasses. She was quiet and stayed at the outer edge of the group. She would smile politely as the rest of us broke into peals of laughter at some joke. I knew she was shy, and so I made a point to talk to her one on one which was easier for her. She was a sweet person. The overall atmosphere was supportive and friendly.

The next day, Jane and I were assigned to do admissions. She oriented me as to how it should be done. After the patient changed their clothes into patient gowns, a series of questions were asked to assess their safety for surgery. Each of us had a list of patients in the order of their time for surgery and we used it to call them to the dressing rooms. As I scanned the list, I noticed the names of the surgeons. My eyes stopped on the name of Dr. Hume, my OB/GYN doctor. He knew all about my mental health history as he was directly involved with my post-partum manic event. What would happen if he saw me? I found myself looking around corners and down halls to be sure he wasn't going to see me. Though my health history should be confidential, there was still that nagging apprehension. Nothing was said that day and I breathed a sigh of relief. As days passed, I could no longer avoid seeing Dr. H., but he never displayed any sign of recognition. I knew this was an act of kindness on his part. Had he engaged in conversation with me, it could have introduced questions that I wanted to avoid. He had saved my little boy, Patrick, in the delivery room, for which I would be forever grateful, and now he was saving my job, too.

By the time I had worked for a month, my son's first birthday was on the horizon. For the first time in all these months, I could plan to spend some money on his presents and his party. He was walking and climbing and so I bought him a Fisher-Price popper that he could push and little colored balls would pop up and down. The house was decorated in crepe paper and balloons and Mark, my sister-in-law and her children, Mark's parents, and my parents and little sister were invited to this party. They all gave Patrick their undivided attention and more gifts. He reveled in the play and his face was soon covered in frosting as he tasted his first birthday cake. Little blonde ringlets bounced as he ran around going "pop pop pop". I finally felt like the parent I had wanted to be from the beginning.

On a Monday morning in the first week in June, I was busy doing blood draws in the waiting area and around the corner on a surgical gurney came a familiar face. There under the white sheet lay Mrs. Rogers in her hospital gown awaiting her turn for surgery. She had been one of my favorite nursing instructors and a good friend who had been there for me after Sophia's suicide. I should have run to her bedside and caught up with her life, and shared mine, but that same fear that kept surfacing rose up again. Had the psychiatric nursing instructors that had seen me as a patient shared this information with her? I couldn't take the chance. I walked by her as if she wasn't there and felt a twinge of sadness that I felt the need to do it. Hiding this secret was becoming more difficult all the time.

By August, we all were working like a well-oiled machine. We were gathered at the nurse's station in the recovery room around a large desk area doing our charting. Two patients remained, but they were sleeping quietly and were stable so we whispered back and forth. Soon, Helen walked up to us and handed each of us two pages of questions to answer before we left for the day.

"What's this, Helen?" I inquired.

"We need to do histories and physicals on all of you, for insurance purposes."

"When do you want these to be done?"

"Do them now, and turn them into me before you leave. The doctors will review them along with the nurse supervisor and we will do the physicals tomorrow."

I felt a tightening in my chest. Had I divulged my secret without being aware? Had one of my fears been realized? My heart was pounding and I was sure everyone could see anxiety written on my face. I did my best to calm down. Slow deep breaths. Keep your eyes on the page and don't look at anyone. We each began to answer the questions as instructed. Jane stood next to me. Then I came across the inevitable question. Do you have any history of mental health issues? I stared at it. Thoughts swarmed through my mind like bees in a hive. Should I lie? I could. They would never know. But this was not just a job. These people were my friends. I knew that I would have to come clean someday. The suppressed history had taken its toll. I answered yes.

"Diana, you're supposed to be serious," Jane said with a big smile.

"I am being serious."

"You are?" she whispered.

"Yes, I'm manic-depressive," I whispered back without meeting her gaze.

"Oh," Jane said, pausing. "It'll be alright."

"I sure hope so."

With sweaty palms, I took my questionnaire to Helen, laid it on her desk with barely a glance and strode away. Tomorrow would tell the tale. That night was filled with restless sleep.

Friday was the next day, and came quietly, but with great gravity. I walked in the employee entrance, put my purse away, took my stethoscope, and went to the ice machine to join in the morning ritual of making ice bags. I was completely quiet. The chatter and joking went on without me. Jane continued to smile quietly and met my gaze with a slight smile, without any hint that she felt differently about me. As we went into the recovery room, the busy day kept my mind occupied so that the impending confrontation didn't take hold of my thoughts. Then as the recovery room began to empty out, Helen came in to take each one of us for our physical. I silently wished I could get this over with. Much like someone in front of a firing squad, eventually a person just wants the inevitable to be done.

Finally, Helen came for me. I followed her with my gaze down to the floor. I walked into one of the exam rooms that the doctors had, and the supervisor Elizabeth and Doctor Franks stood waiting holding my form. The doctor did a cursory exam of heart and lungs and asked questions about my thyroid, which I answered as honestly as I could.

"What kind of mental illness do you have?" the doctor asked.

"I'm Manic-Depressive."

"Are you taking medication?"

"They took me off lithium because it caused a goiter. I have not had any symptoms return since they stopped it. Dr. P., my out-patient psychiatrist, decided to leave me off it but I continue to go there for counseling."

"I see. Okay, thank you."

I stood as though waiting for an event to occur. "You can go, now," he said again.

I exhaled a small sigh and turned and walked out the door. I returned to the recovery room nurse's station, and Jane sidled up next to me.

"Well, how did it go?"

"It went alright," I said as she gave me a hug.

"I told you so."

Acceptance is so often taken for granted. When I was younger, before my first manic event, it never even occurred to me that I would ever do anything that might separate me from others out of a sense of shame. There was a line of demarcation. I would never be the same carefree person again, who took approval as an established fact. I had seen things like this in others who had experienced a life-changing event. I had found people who would accept me as I was. They would become my new friends. I was back to my career and my life as a wife and mother and it was as though I had been resurrected into a new life.

CHAPTER TWENTY-THREE

MOVING WEST

The phone was ringing as I chased a little toe-headed Patrick through the two-bedroomed house, trying to hold him still long enough to get his clothes on him. Finally, I released the squirmy two-year-old long enough to pick up the receiver.

"Hello, this is the Dodds residence."

"Hey, Diana, Larry set up a test line and so we can talk all we want as long as we don't hang up."

"Cheryl?"

"Yes. I've been feeling lonesome for ya, and so Larry set up this connection so we could talk all we want."

"Can I just grab Patrick and get his clothes on him? I have his breakfast ready and I can put him in the high chair."

"Just don't hang up, and I'll wait for you."

Larry, Cheryl's husband, worked for the phone company. Cheryl got lonely for family from time to time and we would talk on the phone. I had no idea that this conversation would last all day. We each had things to do, but as long as we didn't hang up the phone, we could continue our conversation. The underlying reason for this conversation soon became clear. Cheryl knew that I was not happy in my circumstances in Wichita, and she wanted Mark and I to move to Washington State. Cheryl and Larry and their two boys had moved there several years previous to this call. The thought of being free from the constant pressure being brought to bear by my father-in-law, and getting away from a painful time in my life, made me want that, too. I had tried to make inroads with Jack, Mark's dad, so I could be accepted by his family, but nothing had improved.

When Mark and I were first married, I found out his parents were soon to celebrate their twenty-fifth wedding anniversary. I bought a silver candy dish as a gift for them. Neither Mark nor Susan had planned anything for them. Jack thanked Mark and ignored me. Even having Patrick, whom Jack loved dearly, did not change his response to me.

I had traveled to Washington State a year before Patrick was born. The country around Bellingham, Washington was some of the most beautiful I had ever seen. I had loved mountains and forests from the time I was a young child. My family had camped in the Rocky Mountains many times, as they were only 200 miles from Goodland. We had even spent a couple of weeks in the Black Hills of South Dakota.

The first time I saw the Pacific Ocean, I discovered another love of mine. The power of ocean waves crashing against large rocks sending spray across my face was a new thrill. The great shimmering expanse of the ocean seemed to go on forever. The pinks, oranges, and pale purples of sunset on the Pacific were love at first sight. I was enthralled.

"Hey, what are you up to?"

"Well, I'm trying to get a little ornery boy to stop long enough to eat."

"Oh, is he being a pill?"

"Always."

"What's going on with you?"

"Oh, just lonely I guess. Larry is working in Seattle this week."

"So, it's just you and your boys?"

"Yes, I sure wish you lived up here. We would have so much fun. We could go up in the hills or out on the ocean."

"I would love that. It's so beautiful up there."

"Mark could go fishing with Larry." The conversation went on from there.

Soon, after this all-day phone call, the campaign to win Mark over to our point of view regarding moving west began. Mark knew that I was unhappy in our current situation, and he knew it had a lot to do with his dad's ongoing interference in our lives. He walked in the door after a long day at work.

"Hi, honey, how was the unit today?"

"Crazy like usual. Dr. F. made rounds and we would stop outside each patient's room, and he would quiz me about the patient's name and family and then he would go in the room: 'Hi, Mr. so and so how's your daughter such and such.'

"You make him look good."

"I know. He calls me one of his girls."

"One he couldn't get along without."

"What did you and Patrick do while I was at work?"

"Cheryl called on a test line that Larry set up. We talked all day."

"The whole day? What did you talk about?"

"We talked about how wonderful it was to live there. She said there's all kinds of good fishing up there. I miss the mountains. The Cascades are even more beautiful than the Rockies."

"Well, that's what you said when you came back from there. What are we having for supper?" he asked as he changed the subject. This diversion from my quest to win Mark over to the idea of moving didn't deter my desire.

Jack continued his campaign of interference by deciding that we needed to have the oil changed in my car without asking us. A truck pulled up outside our rental home, and before I knew what was happening, a tow truck was hauling my Chevy away. Fortunately, I saw the name of the garage on the side of the truck. I called Mark at work, and he was just as surprised as I was. Jack had decided that we needed to have our spark plugs changed without discussing it with us. Unfortunately, the people that Jack hired for this service also destroyed the spark plug wires. Jack didn't pay for this, we did.

Every Wednesday evening, we were expected to arrive at Mark's parent's house. Jack and Dorothy would sit in matching recliners at one end of the room and Mark would sit on the couch, and I either sat next to him or I wound up in what they called the "Monk's" chair. I soon determined that we were there for cross-examination. Every decision that Mark and I would make would be taken apart and discussed. I didn't feel the necessity of being second-guessed. I had determined my life since I was 17 years old, but Mark, on the other hand, had not. Mark had told me that his father had nearly been bankrupted twice and that he lived without a phone from time to time as a child because they couldn't pay the bill. Dorothy, his mother, was now successful in real estate, but I still didn't think they had the right to dictate our lives.

When there was a get together of Mark's grandparents, the Gillespies, or his half-sister Susan's grandparents, the Shepherds, I would hear Jack make hurtful remarks about them on the way to the occasion and on the way back. I often wondered how Dorothy could listen to this abuse without saying anything, since she loved both sets of grandparents. I would stifle my own thoughts about his remarks for the sake of peace in the family, but it was like torture. How did Mark live with this situation all his life?

Each time Mark and I would come home from a family event the discussion would begin.

"Mark, what was your father's problem tonight?"

"I don't know."

"We were late getting to your nephew's birthday party and so we were just trying to sneak in without disrupting anything. Your dad had a conniption about us not stopping in the middle of your nephew opening his presents to say hello to Jack. We weren't trying to be disrespectful. Susan said I didn't understand him, and she's right, I don't."

"I know."

"You know, but you never stand up to him," I said in frustration.

Cheryl's suggestion to move weighed on my mind more and more. I would talk to Mark about possibly moving there and he would not argue the point with me. He would just get quiet as I extolled the virtues of living in Washington State. The subject found its way into nearly every day's conversation. "Possibly," was Mark's answer.

"Let's pray about it." I was certain that God agreed with me.

I sent a letter to the state of Washington to see what would be required to get a nursing license in that state. I got 2 copies of the information. The form had many questions and one of them of course was about any history of mental illness. I knew that I must be honest, or risk losing my license all together. The answer yes to the mental health question required a detailed explanation. I wrote out my history as a psychiatric patient in the hospital and my care after I was discharged. I went to my counsellor to ask her to write a letter on my behalf. I suggested to Mark that if I could get a nursing license in Washington State, that would indicate that moving was what God wanted us to do.

A couple of weeks later, Mark and I were at a camp that the church was putting on, where I was functioning as the camp nurse. Mark came down to camp with Patrick every day. We walked out under the summer sky full of stars and warm fragrant air.

"Mark, if I get a license in Washington State, I think it is because God wants us to go there."

"Well, time will tell," he said, staring off into space.

"We could start looking for jobs up there, don't you think?"

"We will need them before we can leave here," Mark replied.

"I wish I could take my job from Minor Surgery Center with me. I love it there, but I just need some space from your dad."

Mark sat quietly next to me in my cabin at camp, and made no reply, which I assumed meant that he was in agreement with me.

"It's beautiful there. You'd love it," I said to reinforce my argument. Assumptions can be dangerous, and I was making life-changing assumptions because it was what I wanted so much.

A month passed and one day I opened the mailbox and there was an envelope from the department of licensure of the State of Washington addressed to me. I held it in my hands like a bomb that might explode, afraid to open it. Again, I was being judged. What would they say? Would I ever not be judged again? I doubted that. I had taken a risk in divulging this information to the licensure board and had placed hope in my peers. Would my risk pay off?

I opened the envelope and breathed a sigh of relief as I saw a new nursing license with my name on it. In the weeks that followed, so did a Washington State license for Mark. I called Cheryl to tell her the news and she gave me information from the local hospital want ads. What followed were jobs in Bellingham at the local hospital. I called Cheryl and she agreed to come out and help us pack up and move. Mark and I gave notice at our respective jobs and began the process of filling containers. Mark had gone through this whole process without verbalizing any questions or complaints, but he also had not shown excitement at the prospect of leaving Wichita. Wichita was not only his home, but had been home to both sides of his family back as far as his great grandparents.

Cheryl arrived on a plane at the Mid-Continent Airport and the very next day she and I were busy boxing up our belongings and talking and laughing together. I had a sense of being released from a dungeon of sorts, a place where I was not wanted. Hours passed as Cheryl and I wrapped dishes and folded clothes in the basement of our little rental house. I didn't notice for quite a while that Mark was not packing. I went up the stairs from the basement, into the kitchen, and he was sitting at the dining room table with a sad look on his face. The difference in his demeanor sent a surge of fear through my mind. Mark had never truly left home before. I hoped he was just working through his feelings on the matter. We only had two weeks before we were to start our new jobs and so we needed to be getting things done.

"Mark, are you alright?"

"No, I'm not alright." A long pause passed at a glacial pace. "I don't want to move."

"What? But we have already given up our jobs and agreed to take those two jobs in Bellingham!"

"I know! I'm not going," he said in a tone of defiance and his eyes flashed and the muscles in his face tensed.

The reality that I had been deluding myself into believing that I would ever get away from this difficult situation hit me like a brick wall. I nearly staggered as I walked downstairs and threw myself on a pile of laundry and began to cry. The crying turned into the most intense wailing that I had ever had, like the stopper to a bottle of pain that had been thrust into the sky. All the frustration and sadness from the last six years burst out. Cheryl came to me and tried to comfort me, but I knew that nothing that she said would make any difference. Mark was adamant and unmoved by my tears.

Cheryl berated Mark for changing his mind at the last minute and he walked out the door. After I had cried myself dry, I slowly climbed the stairs and dropped onto the couch fully emotionally spent. I just sat there and felt numb. Cheryl made Patrick something to eat and got him ready for bed, and then called her friend in Bellingham and told her about what had happened. Cheryl was angry and she told her friend, Karen, that she would have to be her sister. I felt that remark deep in my soul. I was caught between my sister and my husband.

After a couple of hours Mark returned. He walked straight in the door and was headed to the bedrooms in the back.

"I've come for Patrick," he said.

Cheryl moved so that she stood between Mark and Patrick's room.

"I don't think Patrick is going anywhere," my sister said.

"I need to take him to my parent's house."

"No," Cheryl said firmly. Mark hesitated. Cheryl's intense stare, with her hands on her hips and firm tight lips, intimidated him.

"I will stay here with you. I hate it here, but I will stay with you," I said quietly.

"Diana, don't give into him," Cheryl pleaded.

"I can't win, Cheryl. If he wants to divorce me he would win and I would never get custody of Patrick. I will stay here so I can keep my son. Mark, I want you to call the elders and see if we can reconcile our differences."

"I will call them," Mark said and quietly turned and exited out the front door.

The next day, Mark and I met with the church elders. We each took turns voicing our frustrations. I talked about Mark not standing up for me with his parents and Mark said he felt pressured into moving when he didn't want to move. I did my best to explain the problem as I understood it and Mark did as well. I reiterated that I was willing to stay in Wichita. After two different meetings with the elders, we called our previous jobs and managed to reclaim them, and notified the hospital in Bellingham, Washington that we had changed our minds. I was right back where I had been before, with barely a ripple to evidence the conflict, except for my pervasive sadness. Cheryl left for her home.

Two weeks after Cheryl flew back to Seattle from Wichita, we were back at our lives as they had been before. One day when Mark came home from work, he had a change of heart.

"Diana, I've changed my mind. I want to move to Washington State," Mark told me.

"I don't care. I don't believe you. I'm not going anywhere."

"But I mean it Diana."

"Mark, you are going to have to prove to me that you mean it. I'm not going through this again. You know that you will get a lot of pressure from your dad. Let's see how you do over the next year."

Within the day, Mark told his dad about our plan to move in a year's time. Every week of that year, Jack would get together with Mark and try to convince him not to go. He would use every argument he could think of. As an example, he told Mark that he had talked to a Native American psychiatrist, who said that I needed help and not to move. Jack knew that I was fascinated by Native American culture and had often gone to pow-wows at the Mid-America All Indian Center. Neither Mark nor I knew of any Native American psychiatrist and certainly I had never met one.

The one thing that Jack did not do to try to change our minds was to change his behavior toward us, which would have made a difference. The behavior continued of Jack going out the back door as I came in the front door, which he had done long before he even knew me.

As the year began to close, it occurred to us both that we did not have a down payment for a house. The year had given us more time to think things through. My dad had been fighting prostate cancer for several years and I was concerned about leaving him behind. My parents had a 4-bedroom house in Goodland 300 miles away and just the two of them lived there. The house was paid for. Mark and I made an agreement with my parents to live with them in Goodland for a year and save what we didn't have to spend in rent towards a down payment on a house. We would pay our portion of expenses otherwise.

Mark did not waver once over that year. He had stood up under a lot of pressure and had come out on the other side. Mark told me about the day he left Cheryl, Patrick, and I at the house the previous year. He had gone to his parents' home and his father had already been on the phone to a divorce lawyer and had sent Mark back to get Patrick. I had suspected it, but now I knew that Jack would never stop until he split us apart.

The day finally came for us to move to Goodland, and Jack actually sent some men over to help pack up our belongings into a U-Haul truck. Three different times that day Jack came by to check on the progress. Finally, he opened the screen door and walked into the living room. I was folding clothes and placing them in a box at the back of the house.

"Are the men getting your things packed?" Jack queried, remaining where he stood.

"We are working together. We should have it done by late this afternoon."

"I can see that."

"Thank you for sending the help."

"I will pray for you," he said in a condescending tone as he turned to walk out the front door.

"That's alright, I can pray for myself."

After my last day at Minor Surgery Center, my co-workers gave me a going away party. The U-Haul was in the parking lot and Mark was in our car, and Dorothy, his mother, was in her Pontiac with Patrick and our cat because she had air conditioning, and because she wanted us to know she was there for us. Mark drove our 74 gold Valiant. I climbed into the cab of the truck as I knew how to drive a standard transmission and Mark did not. As I fired up the engine, I turned on the radio and out came "Believe it or not I'm walking on air, I never thought I could feel so free-e-e!" I burst into song and pulled onto Hillside and headed out of Wichita for good.

CHAPTER TWENTY-FOUR

COMING HOME

The truck lurched up the driveway to my parent's turquoise ranch-style home. The large cement porch wrapped around the front of the house from the front door to the side door with metal posts holding up a cover over the porch. The engine of the truck backfired a couple of times after I turned it off. I felt like the truck myself. The drive had been very hot, since there was no air conditioning, and it took 7 long hours. Dorothy pulled up in her 73 gold Pontiac, which we lovingly called "the lumber wagon" because of its length. Patrick had ridden with his grandma Dorothy because her car had air conditioning. As soon as the Pontiac stopped, Patrick opened the back door and climbed out of the car and came skipping up to me, as the sun reflected off his blonde hair, which had his first little boy haircut. He had napped along the way, so he was rearing to play. Our gold Plymouth Valiant pulled up behind the Pontiac with Mark behind the wheel.

"Sis, I talked with Frenchie next door, and he says you can store your stuff in his garage out back," Dad said as he walked across the porch and picked Patrick up. His worn blue overalls, blue work shirt, and red baseball cap were contrasted by Dorothy's red dress, styled black hair, and gold colored bracelets and high heels.

"Let's take a look inside and see what we need to move in, and what we are going to store. We have a couple of weeks before we start to work at the hospital."

"Hi, Virgil," Mark said as he strode up and shook dad's hand.

"Hello Mark, and Dorothy. Come on in."

"Thank you Virgil, but I have a room at the motel on the highway, and I need to check in."

"How about we go get some supper. I'll tell Elva, and we'll show you the way to the motel."

"Well, hello Dorothy. It was awful good of you to help the kids move. You look tired. Let's get some supper for everyone," Mom said as she stepped out of the side door onto the porch, in a print work dress, black flats, and short salt and pepper hair.

Dad was on his best behavior, but his affection for Patrick was genuine. He put him up on his shoulder and tickled him. Patrick laughed and was thoroughly enjoying the attention. Patrick's grandpas both loved him dearly. I knew being away from Jack would be hard on Pat, so I was glad that Dad was connecting with him so well.

My mother now worked at the Husky Motel where Dorothy had a room, and she helped get her checked in, and then we all walked across the hot asphalt to the Husky truck stop restaurant. The front of the restaurant was filled with large glass windows, and inside there was a counter with revolving red stools, booths that lined the walls, and tables with wooden chairs. We put two tables together and sat down. The menus were on the table with the usual truck driver fare of meat and potatoes. The conversation ranged from the details of our journey from Wichita, to the upcoming job change, and the rest of the time was filled with Patrick's antics around and under the table. Dorothy was gracious, though I knew this was not what she was used to. She was quiet but still made eye contact and smiled slightly. As the pink, orange, and pale purple colors covered the sky, Dorothy and Mark walked to her room, and when she was settled in, he came back and joined us in the Valiant.

We walked in the side door of my parent's house, and went to bed. I bathed Patrick in the bathroom across from his new room, and read him stories until he could finally unwind enough to fall asleep. Mark had gotten into the bed in my old room. I knew he was exhausted and so was I. I fell into bed along with him and was asleep before the clock could tick one more minute.

Dorothy stayed overnight at the motel and Mark, Patrick, and I joined her for breakfast at the truck stop. After breakfast, she stood holding Patrick's hand, while Mark settled the bill. This was the hardest part of our journey away from Wichita. Dorothy had tried to include me in the family, but she had not been raised to go against her husband's wishes. I had always hoped that she might stand up to Jack on my behalf, but that had not happened. She had come to my aid when I was psychotic and she had always been kind, but she joined Jack in his constant questioning of our choices and gave us unsolicited advice. This behavior caused constant uproar between us and threatened our marriage. Still, I had a soft spot for her in my heart.

We walked Dorothy to her car and Mark put her suitcase in the trunk. She hugged us all, especially Patrick, said good-bye with moisture in her voice, and then began her drive home via Interstate 70. This was a huge step for Mark. He had never lived outside of Wichita, or worked in a small hospital, and had never spent more than two weeks with my family at any one time.

The Northwest Kansas Medical Center had a larger name than the hospital indicated. It was a small 50 bed hospital with two of them being an ICU, and two being a CCU. They had long ago torn down the old red brick hospital that I had worked in. The new hospital was built partially because they got federal funds for rehabilitation of Vietnam Veterans, although those veterans never materialized. The hospital had a very substantial physical therapy department and the halls and bathrooms were built for the disabled. For a small community of 5000 people, it was really a fine facility. We drove to the hospital so we could inform them that we were in town and would be there for work in a month, as agreed, and then drove a couple of blocks to the house and came up the driveway. Dad met us on the porch shortly after we arrived.

"Come here, you kids, I want to show you something."

"Alright," I said as I walked into the house and followed him into the kitchen, where Dad stood next to the stove.

"Look at this," Dad said with a grin, as he lifted the top of the stove. I wasn't even aware that the stove could do that, as I had never seen mom do it.

"That is a petrified mouse," Dad said as he pointed to the carcass of a grease-encased mouse. There was at least 3 to 4 inches of putrid grease there. What had made it so important to point out the terrible state of the stove? It implied that Mom was not doing her job.

It made me remember a year earlier, when Mom had flown to Wichita, and had been admitted to the hospital due to excessively heavy menses from going through menopause. She had been experiencing severe anxiety and panic attacks, which was something I had never seen in her. Her OB/GYN doctor had put her on an antidepressant, and was able to control the bleeding by doing a D. and C. The distance from Goodland seemed to stabilize her anxiety and as the antidepressant started working over the next few weeks, she was able to maintain herself at home.

I had noticed that when my parents and my little sister came to visit us in Wichita, they smelled as if they had not bathed for a few days. They weren't around me all the time, but I began to put two and two together. I knew that mom was suffering from depression and perhaps the rest of the family as well. The condition of the house spoke volumes.

I stepped to the refrigerator and opened it to food of all ages stuffed inside. The room where Patrick was staying was clean and so was the bathroom across the hall from it. The second and oldest bathroom was filthy.

"Where is Mom?"

"She's at work until 6." Dad said.

"Well, I think it's time to get busy cleaning around here, and then we can finish moving the rest of our appliances into Frenchie's garage. I'll start on the stove. Mark, why don't you pull up the trash can and start dumping some of the food in the refrigerator, and let's see what we can do here."

Mark and I proceeded to work throughout the day. I also was introduced to the situation with the clothes dryer. Chris had previously told me that she had to reach inside the drum of the gas dryer and spin it manually, while trying to shut the door before everything fell out. I tried it once and that was it.

"Dad, I think we're going to bring our dryer in here. I'm not going to do this with your dryer. That is ridiculous."

"I can fix this dryer," Dad said enthusiastically.

"How long will it take, because we have to catch up on these dirty clothes."

"I need a part, but I'll go get it, and try to have it going this evening. Is that alright?"

"If you could do that, it would save us having to move dryers around."

Dad put on his jacket and walked out the side door and drove off.

The phone rang, and Chris was calling to find out what we were up to, and if we were moved in. During the chit chat, the question of the dryer came up once again.

"Why did you and Mom put up with this situation?" I asked Chris.

"We've been asking him to fix it for 2 years."

"Two years? I would have hired someone to fix it."

"Mom couldn't afford it. Mom pays all the bills except the house payment. Dad pays that, but he keeps the rest in pockets he had mom sew in his underwear." My initial assumption about how dysfunctional and depressed my family was began to be proven correct. I knew that Mom worked 6 days a week, and I also knew that Dad and Chris did nothing to help around the house. Now, I wasn't sure who was rescuing whom.

CHAPTER TWENTY-FIVE

HARD TRUTHS: I

Dad stepped up to help us care for Patrick while we worked, which was a pleasant surprise. I worked day shift and Mark worked evenings. Patrick went to daycare until either my dad or I picked him up. He was not used to being with other children this much and it was an adjustment for him. Dad would soften the blow of being separated from family by taking Pat to the park and then for ice cream. The parks were designated as daddy water tower and mommy water tower by Patrick, after the two different types of water towers in town with nearby parks. Dad and Patrick became buddies. I would ask what they did at the park, and Dad would smile and say that I wouldn't want to know. I knew that Pat was safe, but I knew that he probably did some things at the park that mom wouldn't have let him get away with. I was happy that they were getting along so well. It became obvious that grandsons were easier for him to relate to than the daughters in his own family.

One night, after Mom, Dad, and Patrick were in bed, I went out for breakfast, which was my favorite me-time activity. By the time I got home, it was past my bedtime, but when I walked into the side door, I found Dad sitting up in the family room in his overalls, no shirt, no shave, chain smoking with his hair all eschew.

"What's going on Dad? I thought you would be asleep by now. Don't you work tomorrow?"

"Yea. I was having a lot of pain. I took 5 percojesus but it still hurts."

"What did you take?" Dad threw the bottle at me. It was an over the counter pain medication, but the normal dose was 2. "How long have you been having this much pain?"

"Ever since I broke my arm. You remember, I had to go to Denver for it, because of the bone cancer. Now, I have pain all over. Then I have these dreams where I wake up in my room and I look out the window and it's dark. All of a sudden I feel pain, and dark, sharp, pieces of glass are coming through my skin from the inside out."

"Oh, Dad, that must be such a frightening dream."

"It happens every night." He dropped his head, as tears dropped onto the floor. "I don't want to die."

"Of course you don't. I think it's time to contact Dr. L. and do some more extensive testing. We need to get you some pain relief, first off."

"I suppose I'll have to."

"I'll be there with you."

"Okay."

"Do you think you can go back to sleep?"

"I'll try."

After talking with Dad about the pain that he had, and that it was worse at night, Dr. L. felt that Dad needed a full bone scan, and admitted Dad to the hospital to achieve it. As the results came in, and Dr. L. reviewed them, it became clear that a meeting must happen. He called the family to the hospital cafeteria dining area the next day to discuss the results of the scan. Doctor L. sat down at one of the tables in the dining room. Dad, Mom, Mark, and I sat at adjoining tables to get the verdict of Dad's bone scan. I knew it would not be a good report because we knew that the prostate cancer had already metastasized to his right upper arm. Dad had a spiral fracture in his right upper arm from a fall when he was reading meters for the city of Goodland a year before we moved. An x-ray of the arm showed cancer all around the fracture. He had gone to Denver to see an orthopedist to see if they could stabilize the fracture so he could receive radiation to the fracture. Before he left, his brother, Glenn who was an elder in our church, came and laid hands on him for healing. When he got to the hospital in Denver, they repeated the x-ray and found that miraculously the fracture had begun to heal. That healing had given my parents a false feeling of hope.

Dr. L. was a kind and gentle man. He paused, smiled slightly, and looked each of us in the eye.

"Mr. Middleton, I've reviewed your bone scan. Unfortunately, it shows that the cancer has spread to most of the bones in your body."

"What can we do about that?" I queried

"We can give your dad intravenous Stillbesterol. It is a female hormone that will slow the growth of the tumors because they are sensitive to testosterone. This therapy will buy you more time, Mr. Middleton, and should help reduce the bone pain you are having. The degree of spread of your cancer will lead to your death, however."

The air was pregnant with the shock that my parents were experiencing. We all sat silently for several minutes.

"I will give you stronger pain medication, and I will do whatever I can to keep you comfortable and make your remaining time the best we can."

We stood and each one of us shook Dr. L.'s hand and began to walk silently back to Dad's hospital room as we let this information sink in.

I feared what my Dad might do because of this information. When Dad reached his room, the first thing he did was call Uncle Cecil and asked him to take all the guns out of our house. Later that evening, as the hormone therapy infused, Dad complained of burning throughout his body. He had fought prostate cancer for 10 years, and now he was losing. I turned on the nurse's call light and he was given pain medication, and when the infusion was completed, he was finally able to sleep.

Dad had dropped a lot of weight since the cancer had reached his bones. His once full, thick, brunette hair now was thin and turning gray. He looked like a shadow of himself. As time went by, Dr. L. did some abdominal x-rays and then told me that Dad had a tumor that was pressing against the outlet of his right kidney to the point that it could not empty any longer. This tumor would also increase with time. The hard truth was that Dad was 59 years old and riddled with cancer.

CHAPTER TWENTY-SIX

TIMETABLE

The next day after I became aware of my father's abdominal tumor, I was working day shift at the Goodland hospital. Dad was still receiving treatment there. The charge nurse assigned me to his hallway, which made him my patient. I didn't think that it was a good idea, but she was in charge, and I needed my job. Dad shared his room with another man.

He lay in his bed with his ventilated hospital gown, which actually made him look even smaller than his cancer had already made him. His eyes were bloodshot and his face was covered in grey stubble. The remnants of his breakfast were stacked on his bedside table. He had eaten bites, but most was uneaten. I listened to his lungs, heart, and abdomen, and quizzed him about nausea and pain, but he denied them. I proceeded to assess my other patients as well and then prepared to pass my first round of medications. I noticed Dad talking on the phone as I stepped down the hall. Soon the call light went off, and I entered to see what was needed.

"How do I know you aren't poisoning me?" he asked as he glared at me.

"What?" I said with disbelief.

"I don't believe that medication you brought me was for me. Show me the chart."

"Why would I give you something you shouldn't have?"

"I don't know. Why would you?"

The other man in the room stared at both of us. I was flustered, but proceeded to go and get my dad's chart and take it to the bedside.

"Here, you can read it for yourself," I said, determined to convince him of my sincerity.

"How do I know that you didn't change this chart?"

"I would never do that."

The rest of the shift continued in the same vein. Dad challenged everything I did and said, and was making it impossible for me to care for him. There was no other staff to save me during that shift, but when the 3pm-11pm shift arrived, so did Vernice. Vernice was the widow of one of Dad's best friends and an RN that I had worked alongside in the past. She had many years of experience. I had worked with her as a nurse's aide long ago. Dad trusted Vernice completely. As soon as I saw her, I began to cry. My professional demeanor dissolved, as I explained to her what had been happening.

"You should never have been assigned to your dad in the first place," she said. I shook my head in agreement. "You go finish your charting and go home, and I'll take over with him."

I was so hurt and angry as I left that day. Why would I do anything to hurt him? He should have known me better than that. Was this some kind of grief reaction? I had no idea what had turned him against me. I entered the house, ran to my bedroom, and fell across my bed and sobbed. I was torn between my own grief at losing him and the anger at being treated so unfairly.

Later that evening, I received a phone call from Dad. He was pleasant and said nothing to explain his behavior. This change in his demeanor was like Jekyll and Hyde. He asked me to take him to a movie, as Doctor L. had given him a pass for the evening. I wanted to strike out at him and give back to him what he had given me all day, but I knew he was a dying man, so I tried to be patient with him. Grief expresses itself differently for each person. Mom and I arrived at the hospital and I went in to get him. He walked out the door of the hospital with me in an upbeat manner. I knew I owed that to Vernice.

We went and saw the movie "Annie". It made me sad as I knew that my dad and my life with him would not have the happy ending that I had seen in the movie. We drove back to the front of the hospital and Dad began to open the car door. I finally asked him what had made him so angry earlier in the day.

"I got a phone call from your father-in-law, after I received that hormone medication. I was in a lot of pain. He accused me of trying to steal your things. I thought you'd asked him to call me."

"What would make you think that? Don't you know me at all? You and mom are helping us by letting us live with you. We appreciate your help." Dad didn't reply to my comment. He acted as though his explanation should suffice.

The anger that I felt toward my father-in-law and my own father was immense. I didn't understand why my father didn't trust me. He had been the one so proud of me for becoming a nurse, and now he thought I would use my knowledge against him. When I saw Mark later, I told him what his father had done. He knew nothing about it and apologized for him. I told him that it was not him who needed to apologize. Neither of us could fathom what Jack got out of his behavior.

Doctor L. let Dad go home after his IV Stilbesterol the next day, and gave him the oral form to continue at home. Dad knew he could no longer work his job for the city, but a few months earlier, he had dug up the whole back yard to grow the largest garden that we had ever had. He planted things that he had never grown before and it grew and produced more than any garden I had ever seen. This was as close to being a farmer that he would ever be. He returned to it and seemed more at peace there. The thought that he had missed out on the one thing he wanted most in the world made me sad for him. I bought a canner and canned everything that

I could that came out of the garden. He was proud of it, and in spite of his treatment of me at work, I was proud of him.

One day, when we were both in the garden, I decided that it was appropriate to talk with Dad about the end of his life, which was coming faster than I wanted. I needed to know what he needed from me.

"Dad, I know that this is a difficult subject, but I think we need to talk about where you wish to spend your remaining time. I will stay with you wherever you decide you want to spend the rest of your life. Do you want to die here in Goodland, or do you want to go out to Bellingham, Washington with Cheryl and Chris?"

He paused, and I knew he was calculating the depth of this decision. There were generations of his family in this portion of Kansas and all but one sibling lived here.

"I want to go out to Washington," he said adamantly.

"Then that is what we will do," I said putting my hand on his shoulder. "I will call Cheryl and see if she can help us pack up, and perhaps our church might help."

"I need to get the white truck up and running."

"I'll talk to Lloyd and Norman from church and they can help you get that truck going."

Dad contacted my cousin, Edward, to offer to sell him his inheritance. Grandma had what was called a joint tenancy deed. That meant that when Grandma died, the farm would be divided up among the children, but would remain hers until then.

Edward gave my dad money in exchange for what Dad would eventually inherit. This would pay for a home for my parents when they got to Washington State. I knew that this meant that he was letting go of his life and dreams. He had given up everything for the farm, and now he was giving it up to die where his daughters would live. Cheryl arrived at the end of August of 1982. She and her husband, Larry, had bought a house for Dad and Mom with the money from our cousin Ed, so we would have a place to live when we arrived in Bellingham.

Mark and I continued to work and when we weren't, we helped Cheryl to pack up the house. My parents had lived in their house for nearly 28 years, and so there were many things to pack and many things that would have to be left, to be able to move it across the country to Washington State from northwest Kansas.

Dad busied himself trying to get his white Dodge pickup ready to tow a trailer full of belongings. Lloyd Peters and Norman Gordier from our church, who taught auto mechanics at the local vocational school, came over after teaching school all day for several nights to help him rewire the truck and get the engine tuned up. This impressed my dad, and for once, he saw my church in a positive light. Many of the membership would show up to help pack and load the items that we had decided to take along. Mark and I gave up some of our furniture to make room for other items, as did Mom. Dad gave up some of his choicest engine parts for friends. There was sacrifice all around.

CHAPTER TWENTY-SEVEN

HARD TRUTHS: II

On September 24th, we headed out on Highway 24 to the farm with two pickups towing trailers, one car towing another car, and two other cars that my mother and I drove. Dad would lead the caravan and Cheryl would bring up the end. We pulled up the gravel driveway to stop in front of Grandma's house at the farm. On the way up the driveway, I saw Uncle Mike out on the tractor working the field just below the house.

As she always did, Grandma greeted us at the door. I got the usual hug and smile. We walked through the kitchen and dining room to the living room to sit down. Dad sat down on the couch and faced Grandma in her over-stuffed chair, and told her that this would be the last time that she would ever see him, as he was leaving the area and would die in Washington State. She was quiet, but said nothing to him. He sat and waited for a response, but when it did not come, he rose and left the room. Perhaps it was the number of times that Dad had

223

threatened to end his life, that tempered her response. I will never know.

"Grandma, should Mike be on the tractor with his seizure problem? I heard that he had had a seizure at one time, and drove up on the highway on the tractor. I was of the understanding that he didn't drive the tractor anymore because he had epilepsy."

I had seen his medicine in the cabinet in the kitchen when I was looking for a snack months before. He was on two strong anti-seizure drugs. I had heard about the incident regarding Mike winding up on the highway and how close to a tragedy it had been. I thought my question was innocent because this information had been freely shared with me. My grandmother said nothing but turned towards me, and the smile was gone from her face. Her eyes narrowed, her mouth tightened and she glared at me. I had never seen a look like that from her before. I suddenly realized that she saw me as a threat to Mike, which was far from the truth. The last look I got from my Grandma Middleton would be one of hatred and anger. She had been kind and good to me all my life, and it broke my heart. I stood up and left the room, feeling that I had never really known her.

Grandma had some strange ideas about epilepsy. She didn't want anyone talking about it. She seemed ashamed of it. My aunt had tried to change my sister Cheryl from a left-handed person to a right-handed person when she was a little girl living on the farm. She thought being left-handed meant you were a child of the devil, and told Cheryl and Mom that. Now, I knew that Grandma believed all these things. I knew that she would also feel the same thing about my mental illness. I knew that these were things I must let go of. I loved my grandma, but I refused to accept these beliefs about myself or my loved ones.

As I came out the screen door of the farm house, I saw my dad standing outside by the old garage. He motioned me over to him and handed me a letter. He told me that he had come across it in Grandma's house. The letter was addressed to Uncle Mike, and had been written by my grandma during World War II, as the date on the letter indicated. The words that jumped out at me in that letter were the ones that said that she hoped that my dad would be killed in battle. He was in the Pacific theatre of operations at that time. How could a mother say such a thing about her son? My father had done many things that he should never have done, but I never thought my grandmother could do and say such things. This letter was written before he had married my mother. These were hard truths that I had to come to grips with. My father's choice to leave Kansas became crystal clear. I walked across the gravel driveway for the last time, and climbed into the blue 1970 Plymouth and followed the family caravan away from the farm into a new life.

CHAPTER TWENTY-EIGHT

LAST ROAD OUT OF TOWN

The caravan, of two pick-up trucks pulling trailers, one car towing another car, and two individual cars, rolled down the driveway at the farm, and began its way across the country. The wind was fierce as Dad's trailer was blown so hard that it lifted off the road on the back wheels, and it took all that dad could muster to keep from rolling over. We drove at an excruciating 40 miles per hour for the 200 miles to Denver. Patrick felt ill and laid quiet and pale in the back of the blue Plymouth. At one point, a highway patrolman outside of Denver pulled Cheryl over. She was driving a car and towing another one behind it. The officer couldn't see the license plate on the car she drove. The rest of the caravan members kept their eyes out for the vehicles ahead of them and the one following behind so we could stay together. Before that officer knew what was happening he not only got my sister's cars but all of us pulled over too. He walked down the line of vehicles and shook his head in disbelief. I'm sure we were the story du jour, after work.

We had told Mom that she wouldn't have to drive in cities or mountains, but of course we lied, because we knew she would have to take the journey whether she wanted to or not. I knew if she was aware of the truth she would balk at the idea. Her father had taken her out one day when she was twenty years old, and before she moved to western Kansas, and taught her to drive in one afternoon. This brief driving instruction was all she ever received and her only driving since coming to Goodland was from the farm to town and back, which was 13 miles out of town. Change is hard for anyone, but we were up-rooting the entire family and moving it over 1600 miles away and Mom would have to do things she never knew she could.

At every gas station along the way, all the modes of transport crossed the air hoses, which set off a myriad of 'ding ding's that most likely made the attendants think they were under invasion. As soon as we came to a stop at the filling station, the hoods of all the cars and trucks went up as Dad went about checking the oil and the engines. He knew what a cross-country trip could do to a vehicle.

As we traveled, we not only faced high winds, but rain and snow so hard that we had to pull over. The only disaster that we managed to avoid was fire. We kept up a steady pace. There was no time to dilly-dally. Cheryl had promised her son that she would be home for his birthday at the end of the month, and so kept the pressure on to make as many miles a day as we could. Dad was in the lead and my sister, Cheryl brought up the rear. She traveled right behind mom, to help keep her calm and reassured.

Every night when we had found our accommodation, Cheryl would sit with Mom for a couple hours, while mother cried and swore that she couldn't traverse the country any further. Cheryl would listen and hold her as she cried and reassure her that she would stay close behind her and keep her safe. Mark had never traveled this far, either, and she reassured him as well. It became her nightly ritual.

Dad's left leg was almost three times the size of his right one, because his cancer had blocked the lymph nodes for the leg, so that it was not draining back fluid into circulation as it should. How he used the clutch with it, I will never know. In the mountains and cities, that meant a lot of shifting. One day, he missed his turn on the interstate and was heading the wrong way. He made a quick turn, drove the truck and trailer down a ditch and up the other side onto the right road, without skipping a beat. Cancer was taking his life but he was determined to die in the Pacific Northwest and he had finally divorced himself from the long fought-for farm.

The procession of vehicles traveled through Denver, Colorado; Cheyenne, Wyoming; Ogden, Utah; and Portland, Oregon; and finally, the most beautiful stretch of road between Mount Vernon, Washington; and Bellingham, Washington. The cars, trucks, and trailers bounced over speed bumps on the road into Mount Bakerview Mobile Estates. I was surprised that parents in the park weren't out rounding up their children as our horde arrived. We had missed my nephew's birthday by a couple of days, so Cheryl headed for her home to be with him. Meanwhile, Mom, Mark, Patrick, Dad, and I made ourselves at home in the house bought for my parents. As we moved the beds and living room furniture into the three-bedroom house, it was close quarters, but we had survived the longest journey most of us had ever made.

CHAPTER TWENTY-NINE

DON'T GO QUIETLY

October began with Mark and I looking for work. What had been so easy in the mid-1970s when I looked for work in Wichita, had become more difficult in 1982 in Bellingham. In Wichita, when I started as an RN, health care was in the midst of a nursing shortage. The 1982 Pacific Northwest had more nurses than the Midwest, which meant fewer opportunities.

Every day, Mark and I searched want ads and made phone calls to perspective employers. I tried to use up the spare time making a uniform for Mark. As a seamstress, I was a miserable failure and spent a lot of time tearing out the stitches I had just put in. I was somewhat apprehensive about the work situation, but with our work history, I was sure we would finally prevail.

Dad continued his bouts of irritability and pointed them with increasing viciousness at Mom.

"What are you trying to do, kill me? I can't eat that, the smell makes me sick," he once proclaimed.

"I'm sorry, Virgil, what sounds good to you?"

"I want stewed tomatoes."

"I don't know how to make them."

"You don't know shit."

And so the turmoil went on day after day.

I managed to talk Dad into going to a cancer specialist. He needed an implanted central line, which could be used to draw blood samples, give blood, and also could be used for medications that would otherwise hurt small blood vessels in the arms. He refused to allow the doctor to do that. Dr. D. the oncologist offered him a very slim chance with a drug trial for prostate cancer. Dad agreed to try it. Over the previous few months, he had lost a great deal of weight and his hair had started to turn grey, but this drug took more, because of the nausea and vomiting. He started losing his remaining hair, and what remained was wispy and nearly white. My little sister, Chris, had been living with Cheryl for several months before we arrived and had not seen Dad during that time. When she did finally see him, she nearly came to tears at the sight because he truly was a shadow of himself.

Mark and I would take Dad out on rides as he became weaker. We drove up on Mount Baker, a snow-capped, inactive volcano near Bellingham. We would stop just a short distance below a place called Nooksack Falls, and he would get out of the car and take in the sight of a forest of evergreens and the painted leaves of the alder trees. At the bottom of the narrow valley was the dark green, shimmering Nooksack River. I couldn't help but think that he would have been so much happier here than fighting for land that would never be his. At 59 years of age, the possibilities for his life were coming to a close.

One night, Dad kept Mom awake all night yelling that Mark and I were trying to steal everything they had. I knew he was saying this because Mark's father, Jack, had accused my parents of stealing our possessions. To have my father ranting at me was one thing, but to have him accuse my husband, who had been nothing but patient and kind to him, was another. Patrick was only four years old, and he loved his grandpa who had played with him oftentimes, so this was confusing. I could deal with his moods, but it was not fair to expose my family to them constantly. At some point, my compassion for Dad dissolved into anger and frustration.

Within two days, we bought a mobile home of our own, placed less than a block from my parents, and we moved out as soon as we could. I hated to leave Mom with that situation. She would have to deal with Dad all day and all night, and he would not let her leave him. I reassured my mom that I was available to help her, and spent much of my spare time doing just that. My brother-in-law was able to calm him, and he would step in to give Mom a reprieve.

Our fortunes changed as Mark and I found jobs in the hospital in Mount Vernon, Washington, just 28 miles south of Bellingham. Mark and I worked opposite shifts to allow more time for Patrick to be with one or the other parent. Mark worked the 3pm to 11 pm shift on an orthopedic/psychiatric floor. I worked two months 11pm to 7am and switched to two months 7am to 3pm and then back again on a medical-pediatric floor. The switching made it difficult to know when to sleep, but I managed to get enough. Mark did all he could do to reduce my stress and make sure I slept.

At night, when I was home, I would get phone calls from Mom asking for help. Sometimes she called because Dad was in so much pain that he required a shot of Demerol. The oncology doctor had allowed me to have the injections to give to Dad. There was no hospice in those days. He had a partial bowel obstruction, which made it difficult to eat, and pass stool, which increased his pain, and I would give small enemas. Mother and I would pass each other under the streetlight so that Mom could go be with Patrick while I gave Dad an enema and a shot. This allowed him to sleep and allowed Mom some peace and quiet.

One moist foggy day in December, Dad was able to walk to our house. He wanted to see our new home. At first, Dad was pleasant but soon began one of his time-honored rants. The difference this time was that he was in my home yelling at me.

"That's it, Dad! I know you're very sick and in pain, but I don't deserve being treated this way, and neither does Mom. You are in my house this time, and if you can't behave, you can leave." This felt good to a point, and yet a part of me still felt guilty at yelling at such a sick man.

"I don't know why I behave this way. I'm sorry," he said as he stepped to the kitchen sink and bent over it and began to cry.

"I don't know why you do it either, Dad," I said in a conciliatory tone, "but you are driving away the very people who are trying to help you." I placed my arm around his shoulders and felt the quaking of sobs and realized just how frail he had become.

"Come on, I'll take you home, and try to make you more comfortable."

Dad's last Christmas was held at my home. For a few short hours he seemed at peace and I saw him smiling off and on. My mother sat in my wooden rocking chair in the living room, with her eyes wet with tears. The trip out here, away from everything she knew, and the stress of Dad's behavior and watching her husband fading away, was taking its toll. Mark took pictures of the festivities including a hug and kiss that I gave my dad, which would become a treasure in years to come.

On February 13, 1983, we all gathered at Dad's bedside in the small local hospital. I was still in nursing mode trying to care for him. Dad was so uncomfortable that everything I tried to do seemed to make him more so. After trying to turn him off his back, to his left side, I saw him look past me as if I wasn't there, and a faint smile crossed his face, as he took his last shuddering breath.

An overwhelming wave of grief passed over me as I choked back sobs. I was 29 years old and my dad wasn't supposed to die so soon. Whatever opportunity there might have been to have a different relationship with him was gone forever. I ran to the waiting area and dropped into a chair and buried my face in my hands. One of the nurses that had cared for Dad followed me.

"You did such a good job with him," she said.

"I tried, but it just seemed to make things worse. He suffered so much," I cried.

"He didn't suffer because of you. You were there for him," she insisted, and wrapped her arms around me. I remembered the power of her words at that moment, and years later, when I cared for cancer patients, I passed on her compassion. I had seen death before many times, but never had it come so close to me.

DEATH COMES
By Diana Dodds

Death comes with heavy hand squeezing out each gurgling breath;
Cooling the fire in your heart, until your hands turn cold and damp.

Your eyes look out through heavy lids, with gauzy stare,
and your mouth rests slack jawed.

I sit counting the ticks on the clock, as your life oozes out of you.
Every moment excruciating, melds into the next.

Finally, you gasp your final breath, and your chest falls for its final time.
I feel an arm around my shoulder as I hear, "You were so good with him."

DEPTHS OF GRIEF
By Diana Dodds

How can the world keep on turning? How can people keep on laughing,
working, loving, when the breath has gone out
Of my life?
It should be quiet and still, like the quiet still heart of my love. I am like a
person out of phase, out of time with those around me, and time moves
in measured painful steps.

Take my hand and slowly walk with me.
Halt your hurried pace and hear the echo of my well of grief and linger
there until I can resume the race.

CHAPTER THIRTY

SECOND VERSE

Second verse same as the first!" was something we
shouted as children. The second verse is not always
the same as the first. "If you've seen one, you've seen
them all" is another such saying. It had been nearly 6
years since Patrick had been born. I wanted a second
child, and a normal postpartum period which I had seen
many of my friends and relatives have. I begged Mark
to consider it. After my mental health had been stable
for nearly 3 years, he agreed we could try. Each month,
I would hold my breath until I'd find out that, alas, it
was not to be. I prayed to God and asked him for another chance, another child. We had moved to and lived
in Goodland from August of 1980 to August of 1981 and
then made the move to the Pacific Northwest, but the
answer from God kept being, "No".

Finally, I relented and said, "Thy will be done." We
went to our family physician and he did some testing
on our fertility and, when he received all the results, he

told us that we both had fertility problems and would need to adopt. That was not the answer I was looking for.

Within two weeks of the doctor's suggestion to adopt, I started to have intermittent cramping and spotting of blood. This lasted for fifteen days and ended with the passage of tissue which appeared to me to be a miscarriage. I was heartbroken. The doctor reassured me as much as he could.

Two months passed and I found myself at the doctor for an upper respiratory infection and he announced I was pregnant at last. I wasn't sure who was more surprised, him or me. Looking back, God was wise not to allow that pregnancy while we were living in Goodland, where medical care was less sophisticated. God's answer was not a "No" but a "Not yet".

I was not walking on air like I did when I found out about my first pregnancy. I knew that I was at a higher risk for postpartum psychosis, and so I explained my situation and concerns to my doctor. I knew we would have to be more alert this time. Mark and I watched for problems from day one.

The pregnancy was more difficult physically this time with more nausea, fatigue, and even some rapid heart rate. My mood was not as elevated during this time. I was able to work up until a month before my due date. I had to have a C-section again because of the style of incision they had used in my first C-section which had been an emergency. Because of that, I got to choose my child's birthday, and also make plans for after the baby was born.

The birth went off without a hitch, and was a normal unhurried C-section. I had my mother and sisters available to help me when I went home, and Mark's parents for the first two weeks. I got good sleep, and managed to both breastfeed and bottle feed, which doesn't always work. The planning and support that we had reduced the stress so that it was calm and pleasant. I realized that my first post delivery problems would have been much less severe if I had such a system when Patrick was born. The normal postpartum was finally mine, and I relished the time like fine wine.

I stayed at home for 6 weeks and bonded with my youngest son, Jacob. The hospital where Mark and I worked chose to send a photographer to take my picture for the hospital's county newsletter. He took a picture of me holding Jacob while sitting in a rocking chair at our home. They gave me the picture and it captured that bond that happens between mother and child. In it, I stared down into his little round face and blue eyes and very fine pale blond hair and my smile was mirrored in his face. I remembered that same bond with Patrick and it felt so good to be able to enjoy it again, but without an emotional upheaval. After six weeks I returned to work and Mark and I worked opposite shifts from each other so that there was very little time left where a sitter had to be with the kids.

Days turned into weeks, and weeks turned into years, and my mood held, or so I thought. My youngest son, Jacob, was happy and healthy. He had a sweet disposition and a ready smile and he grew like the proverbial weed. By the time Jacob was 4 years old, I started having frequent health issues. First it was my stomach, which the family doctor treated and it subsided. Then I started to have migraine headaches. He worked me up for them and they subsided. After seeing my doctor every couple of weeks for one thing or another, finally one day in his office, he suggested that the reason I was having so many health issues was because I was depressed. I had been seriously depressed before, and it didn't feel that way to me now. My doctor prescribed Prozac for me. I warned him about what antidepressants had done to me before, by causing me to go back up into mania. He insisted that he would keep a close eye on me.

Before I filled the prescription, I called Mark. Mark now worked on the psychiatric floor at the hospital in Mount Vernon and had been doing so for a couple of years. I had not wanted him to work there, because I was afraid it would bring up too many old memories, but he seemed to thrive there. He certainly understood what the family went through, which made him a great asset. I asked him if Dr. E., a clinical psychologist with a PhD who specialized in psychiatric testing, could do some psychiatric testing for me. The question about depression raised another question. The out-patient psychiatrist in Wichita had told me that I was not manic-depressive when he discharged me from his service nearly 9 years previous to this. I had been taken off lithium at that time, and my mood had seemed stable to me all that time. I would actually be able to read the questions this time; unlike the testing I had received in the hospital during my first psychiatric admission when my vision was affected by medications. Dr. E. agreed, and sent home The Minnesota Multi-Phasic Index, or MMPI.

The test was over 300 questions and many of them were the same question but rephrased. This test was designed to get the truth from people because of the way it repeats questions randomly and in different ways. I worked through it during the evening until bedtime. Mark returned the test to Dr. E. the next day. By 5pm that same day, I got a call from Dr. E. because he was so concerned about the degree of my depression.

"I'm concerned about you, Diana. Your MMPI shows that you are seriously depressed. You need to get help, now," Dr. E. said.

"I don't feel depressed. I've been depressed before, and it doesn't feel the same. I'm tired a lot and have aches and pains all the time is all." I replied.

"How is your sleep?"

"I never seem to be able to get enough. I'm tired no matter how much sleep I get. I hate to get up."

"How many hours are you sleeping?"

"Oh, I probably sleep for 10 hours or more."

"Well, that should be more than enough sleep. How about your appetite?"

"I probably eat too much."

"How about sex?"

"Well, I don't seem to care much for it. I just figured it was because of working and raising kids."

"Do you feel hopeless or helpless?" I paused hesitant to admit what I had actually been feeling. I didn't want to believe that I was sick again.

"Oh, maybe a little."

"Diana, this depression has probably come on very slowly and insidiously and because of that, you didn't notice the same degree of severity or dramatic change in mood that you did after your first manic episode. The swing from mania to depression is more noticeable than swinging down into depression from normal mood. Are you going to get some help?"

"My doctor has already ordered some Prozac."

"You know to be very careful with that, right?"

"Oh, yes, I know very well. Thanks Dr. E.."

"Stay in touch, alright?"

"No problem."

After two weeks on Prozac, I began to feel much less tired. The aches and pains disappeared. I felt increased energy and that made me frightened. Energy and mania are kissing cousins. I called my family doctor and told him that I was feeling much better, but that I was afraid for my mood to raise any further. He concurred with me, and I stopped Prozac that day. I felt so much better, lighter than air, and my worries about the antidepressant causing mania went away.

Since I stopped the Prozac I felt sure I had avoided disaster. Work at the hospital continued as before as well as my family obligations but it was easier because I had energy. There were some new nurses coming to work on my nursing unit because of a change in the types of patients we would have on the floor. Up until this time, we had been medical, pediatrics, and oncology. The nurses joining us had been caring for cardiac patients. They had been nurses for years, but they hadn't cared for pediatrics or oncology patients before. I had cared for cardiac patients many times and felt comfortable with the mix of patients. I felt the need to step up and help them. I would finish my shift, and go out to talk them through their patient's care. My shift usually was done by 4pm at the latest, but with these new nurses, I was spending much more time every day helping them out. It would be 6 to 7pm or later before I would leave. The nurses I helped didn't really seem to appreciate my help, but the patients always came first, in my mind.

In spite of the extra hours at work, I didn't feel tired when I got home. Mark and the boys were starting to get on my nerves though. They weren't loud or anything, but they didn't seem to understand what I needed them to do around the house and it upset me more and more. Irritability is a symptom of mania, which I had not had before. By Saturday, two weeks after the Prozac was stopped, my mood had not bottomed out into depression again, which was a relief, but I felt constantly on edge.

I was still at the hospital at 7:30pm on Saturday and was not stopping except for the bathroom. The hospital supervisor for evening shift entered the nursing lounge as I exited the bathroom there.

"Diana, why are you still here?" she inquired.

"I've been helping the new staff here on the floor."

"Well, they called me, because they feel that you're interfering with their work."

"Interfering? They wouldn't know what to do without my help."

"Nevertheless, you have to go home."

"Go to hell!" I said with my eyes flashing, my hands curled into fists and my face turning red.

"You need to go home," she said sternly, not backing down from me.

I jerked up my work purse and exited the lounge, slamming the door behind me. The thought that I could be fired for such treatment of a supervisor didn't even cross my mind.

Hustling into the house from the car, I slammed the door at home as well. I walked around the house yelling at the top of my lungs. Mark and the boys stayed quiet. Mark knew better than to confront me when I was like this, not unlike my mother, who also kept quiet as long as she could with my dad when he behaved this way.

"I'm going to the pet store," I said matter-of-factly, out of the blue.

"What's at the pet store?" Mark asked.

"I'm going to buy that ferret I've always wanted."

"O.K...? Should I come with you?"

"If you want," I said as I was going out the door. Off to the pet shop I drove with Mark and the boys, and before I left the shop I had a small female ferret and a cage for her. Mark didn't try to talk me out of it. The boys were thrilled with the ferret, and took turns holding her.

I stayed up most of the night going from one partially completed project to another. When I finally did sleep, it was for two hours and then I got up and dressed for work. Shortened sleep time is also a symptom of mania. Before I left the house, I gave Mark a kiss at the door. I hadn't combed my hair or brushed my teeth, but had on a clean uniform. Mark remained calm as I drove away. Like so many times in the past, the floor where I worked was short of nurses. I was on top of my patients' needs and also those of other people's patients all day. I felt highly perceptive and quicker to respond than ever before, which is the seductive part of mania. I was pleasant to the patients and family, but cursed at my co-workers. The charge nurse knew that something was wrong with me, but being short of nurses kept her from acting on it.

After I gave report to the evening shift, I followed my co-workers to the third floor conference room for the monthly unit meeting. My unit supervisor, Melanie, tried to lead the meeting. I interrupted her at every turn. The other nurses couldn't get a word in edgewise and took turns sighing and rolling their eyes. I couldn't imagine what their problem could be. Finally, Melanie ended the meeting and the other staff members left the room.

"Melanie, I noticed some of the other staff were rolling their eyes when I was talking. Is there a problem?"

"Well..., Diana, we are all concerned about you."

Lightning struck my consciousness. Concerned was not good. As Melanie and I walked to the elevator and rode down to the second floor where I worked, Mark was calling the nurse's station there. Unbeknownst to me, he had been working in the background all day to get me a psychiatrist and set up for my admission, which he had seen coming. By the time I walked up to the desk, I was handed the phone. I knew exactly why he was calling.

"Diana, I am downstairs in the chapel with Richard..."

"I know why you're calling. I'll let myself be admitted if you can promise me that my rights won't be taken away."

"I promise that they won't," he said earnestly.

"We'll see," I said skeptically.

Down the hall again, and onto the elevator, and down to the first floor, I marched with purpose. I entered the door of the small chapel and Mark met me at the door. He handed me the patient's bill of rights. I sat down and read it carefully while Mark and his boss, Richard, looked on. I would be testing these rights. The second verse was not the same as the first, and yet it ended in the same place, the psychiatric unit.

CHAPTER THIRTY-ONE

NO MORE SECRETS

Promises were made about my patient rights in that chapel, and afterwards I accompanied Mark, my husband, up to the psychiatric unit where he worked. We stopped at the worn wooden doors that were the entrance to the floor and Mark picked up a phone receiver next to the doors and let the staff know that we were coming in. Once inside the doors, I was greeted by one of Mark's co-workers, Linda. She was about 5 foot 5 inches tall, with straight, short, brown hair. She wore black glasses and was solidly built. The nurses on this unit wore casual clothes rather than uniforms. She wore a short-sleeved light pink dress shirt and light green slacks. I had known Linda outside of this job when Mark's co-workers would gather for social events and she always had the same smile, which made her eyes crinkle. Mark respected her and the fact that she did not bow down to anyone. Now, I saw the same smile as she took my hand and put 4 white pills in it.

"Take this now," she said firmly, handing me a glass of water. I took the pills without a question. Mark escorted me into a room with a desk where my admission would be done.

"What did Linda give me?" I queried.

"That was 4 mg of Ativan." I had given patients 1 mg and it put them to sleep. Ativan was a tranquilizer and often used as a short-term medication to help decrease mania and agitation.

"Mark, I haven't finished charting for my shift! You need to go get some nurse's notes from my patients so I can chart before these medications kick in."

Mark left immediately and returned shortly with sheets of nurse's notes for me. I quickly wrote notes about my care and observations of that day. I handed each one to Mark and had him read them to be sure that they made sense. My notes passed muster, and soon I felt the Ativan slowing down my thinking and I began to feel very sleepy. The remainder of that day and the next have been lost to me ever since.

The second day on the unit, I awoke but remained woozy and a little unsteady on my feet. I attempted to walk up the hallway and found myself weaving from one side of the hall to the other as I made progress towards the nurse's station.

"Diana, we're going on an outing to the beach, do you want to go?" A short, slender, blonde woman named Kathy asked me. "Sure," I said, not fully knowing what I was doing. I was swept up in a group of other patients as we were shuffled to the elevator and down to the 1st floor. I continued to follow along as we went to a van that the hospital used for such activities. I climbed into a seat, and promptly fell asleep. Before I knew it, we were at the beach, and the van doors slid open and people began to pile out. When a person has been cooped up on a psychiatric unit, activities like these are welcome. Fresh, crisp air came off Puget Sound, and everyone pulled their coats tight around them, while waves lapped at the shore. I saw a large piece of driftwood and sat down next to it, on the moist sand. Soon I had fallen over on my side and returned to sleep.

"Diana, it's time to go," Kathy called to me. Time had passed without my awareness of it. I jerked up to a sitting position and eventually got on my feet again. Soon, I weaved my way back to the van, climbed in, and fell back to sleep. I wasn't sure why I had engaged in this activity, but at least one of the promises was kept. I wasn't a prisoner this time.

A new medication, Depakote, had been started. It would take time before it became effective in corralling my moods. They had to raise the dose slowly and meanwhile, the Ativan was used to curb the irritability that had brought me to this point. For the few years that Mark and I had worked in this hospital, I had often come to this psychiatric unit as a visitor. I would come in the door and go back to the charting area next to the nurse's station and visit with the staff as I waited for Mark to walk me to the elevator so I could tell him good night.

Now, I was the patient, and without even thinking, I started to walk back to that charting area, and Linda met me and blocked my path.

"Patients aren't allowed back here," she said.

"I've been back there plenty of times," was my rebuttal.

"Not as long as you are a patient here." I was suddenly confronted with being the "other". Tears welled up in my eyes.

"Well, go to hell then," I said, waving her off and stomping down the hallway. The irritability of mania was raging in my mind. I went to my room and threw myself on the bed, and cried for a very short time, but the energy of mania doesn't allow a person to stay in one place for long. I grabbed a record that Mark had brought me. I went to the group activity room at the end of the hall. I put on a Carol King album and turned it up high. Soon I was singing at the top of my lungs and the sadness evaporated and I was caught up in that moment.

For several days, the irritability continued. It was like an itch you can't scratch. Very little interaction would be sufficient to set off my temper, then I would be upbeat a few minutes later, and then a short time would pass, and I would be crying on my bed. Depression and mania overlapped one another. I had the energy and ill temper of mania, and the sadness and hopeless feelings of depression at the same time. I would discover a new name related to manic-depression called mixed mood.

There was no solid ground under my feet. There was constant shifting and I constantly felt off balance.

"Diana, we are having a class, and you need to go into the dining room and take a seat with the other patients," Linda instructed. I was doing my best to comply and to keep my temper in check. The instructor was a social worker called Steve. He was short and slender with black wavy hair. He was also the person who supervised the unit. He stood at the white board and wrote some of the information for the class, and began to talk. After only a few sentences, I began to make unsolicited comments.

"Diana, you need to be quiet, so the other students can hear," Steve insisted. Again, I felt that I was being unduly punished, and I did my best to be quiet. My feelings were easily bruised at this point. My ability to keep still required all the energy I could muster. I knew things, and he wasn't letting me share my insights with the patients. Again, I began to interrupt his instruction.

"Diana, I need you to shut up, please," Steve demanded.

"Why do you put manic people in a class and expect them to be quiet?" I demanded. "Why don't you wait until I'm better so I can get something out of the class?"

"You need to leave."

"Fuck you!" I shouted. Nurses from the nurse's station came into the room, and I walked off in the opposite direction. I went back to my room, and broke down into sobs. I didn't want to behave this way. It was as though another person had taken possession of me. Although I grew up listening to my father's cursing, which was his first language, cursing wasn't my normal behavior, and I felt a sense of guilt.

Mark was at home with the boys while these things went on at the hospital. He had to take vacation time, because he couldn't work on the unit while I was a patient there. He and the boys would come to visit every evening. That was another one of the promises being met. This night, he called and asked to talk to me. The overflow from my feelings about Steve and his class exploded onto him. After trying to get a word into the conversation, he finally gave up.

"Boys, we won't be going to see Mom tonight," he declared.

By week two of my stay, the Depakote began to make a dent in my moods. I was able to sit for short periods and keep my concentration on a task. There were art projects to do, and some group therapy. I was able to contain my comments until I was asked. I begged Mark to bring the boys, my mother and sisters, and to have the elders of the church priesthood come and do the laying on of hands for healing of the sick. Mark knew it was a test, and he was right. This time, I got to see them all. I was able to talk to them all without losing my temper or interrupting. This was progress. I had not felt like crying for a couple of days. There were daily meetings with Kathy, who was my assigned counselor, and who did recreation as well. She had a son, who was the same age as Jacob, my youngest. She started with discussions about our mutual parenting, and built rapport.

"Diana, there is something that I need to discuss with you."

"Alright."

"We noticed that before you got sick, that you were involved with many things."

"Yes, but I managed them all," I said, feeling rather proud of myself. "I am the contact person for this legislative district for Bread for the World. I have gone to a lot of towns sharing with people about hunger issues."

"Yes, that is what Mark said."

"I am an assistant cub scout leader. I'm trying to help Patrick get to know more kids."

"You do quite a few different activities at your church, too, don't you?"'

"Yes, and I go on field trips with Patrick's class."

"You are going to have to stop doing those things."

"What? Why? Those things are important to me."

"Diana, we think that you are overly involved in things like this and that it adds to your mania. You're going to have to let them go, if you want to get better and go home."

I felt as though the surface beneath my feet had suddenly disappeared and I was gulping for air. Kathy smiled and told me to think about it.

I didn't want to argue with anyone and stir up the beast of mania. I sat myself down at a table in the dining room and began to draw on a piece of paper. I made a cartoon of a woman in the water with inflatable devices holding her up. On each device, I put one of the things that I was being asked to give up. In the next frame, I showed the woman as the balloons began to burst and the woman began to sink. The last frame showed only the hand of the woman as she sank. I realized even as I completed it, that I had used all of the things that I did to keep my self-esteem above the waves. Now, I was again staring into the maw of this illness.

"Diana, Dr. F. needs to see you. Come with me, and I'll have you go into his office."

I followed Linda down the hall to the doctor's office. Dr. F. sat at his desk with a stack of charts. I went in the room, and sat in a chair behind Dr. F. He began to talk, with his back to me.

"I've looked over the nurse's notes, and Dr. B.'s note from your admission, and we have determined that you are bipolar, or manic-depressive," he said curtly.

Dr. F. had put into words what in my mind and heart I already knew, and there it was again, the old feelings of grief. I resented the fact that he told me that news without even looking me in the eyes. If I had been diagnosed with a terminal illness, I would have been shown more compassion. This disease could kill you, as 15%-20% of those diagnosed end their lives. This disease would never go away. My brief years of bliss, at thinking that my first psychiatric experience was a one-time thing, were snuffed out. Dr. F. went on to tell me what he would do with my medications and that a plan was being put in place for a discharge in a few days. I walked out of the office feeling overwhelmed and deeply uncertain of my future. I had had a manic event in front of all my peers. Would I even have a job after this?

I went into the group room and sat down on the couch and the weight of all that had happened rested on me. Soon, Linda came into the room.

"How are you doing?" she asked.

"I'm having a hard time accepting this diagnosis again. I guess I'll have to."

"Diana, did you know that I was diagnosed with cancer at one time?"

"No, Mark never said anything to me about it."

"Being bipolar is not as bad as cancer," she said in an almost condescending tone. I didn't know how to respond to that except to shake my head yes. In my heart, though, I thought that she had no idea what it felt like to have this diagnosis. How could someone who cared for the mentally ill not understand that there is grief over receiving this news? It wasn't a contest about who had been through the most. Linda patted me on the shoulder and left. Tears ran down my face and dripped onto my lap, silently. Eventually, I left the room and headed up the hall for dinner.

As I walked toward the dining room, I saw a familiar face. Dorothy, an LPN who had worked at this hospital long before I came, and who had become a friend, stood at the end of the hall with a bouquet of flowers. Dorothy was about my height, and wore glasses. She had short brown hair and a winning smile. I was so surprised.

"The staff from 2NW asked me to bring you these flowers."

"Really?"

"Sure, and we hope you'll be back to work, soon," she said as she gave me a big warm hug.

"Tell them thanks for me, Dorothy. It means a lot."

I had a lot to think about. In order to get discharged from this unit, I would have to change the way I lived my life. I thought about the cartoon I had drawn. I still felt it was true, but now I had the possibility of returning to work. Kathy, my counselor, came in the room and told me that Dr. H. had given me a pass to go home for a couple of hours with Mark. All the promises that had been made to me, before I agreed to come voluntarily to the psychiatric unit, had been met. It was so different this time.

Upon arriving at home, I immediately began to feel tension that I had been free of for several days. The house looked like a single man and his boys had been living in it. Imagine that. Dirty clothes were strewn about, and toys had been left out. The boys were playing in front of the tv and shouted hello to me as I came in. Neither one of them seemed surprised to see me. Mark was quiet and followed me as I walked around the house. I walked into the kitchen, and in the sink were a lot of dirty dishes. Dirty dishes in the sink was common at our house usually, but now all of a sudden I was seeing red. I picked up a glass and felt the heat of that manic irritability and for just the blink of an eye, I contemplated throwing it through the front window.

"Mark, I'm not ready. Please take me back to the hospital."

"Already? Okay," he said with a question on his face. After we got in the car I told him what I came close to doing. "You're right, you aren't ready yet."

As I came up on the beginning of the third week, the Depakote had reached the peak of its efficiency. I asked for the staff to call Melanie, my floor supervisor, to see if she would meet me. She came up to see me and we sat in a small visiting room.

"Diana, I'm glad that you called me. I knew we would have to have a conversation at some point."

"I appreciate you being willing to come up here to meet with me."

"Can you tell me why you weren't taking your medication?" she asked.

"I had been taken off lithium years ago because of a thyroid goiter. After being off it, the symptoms didn't return, so the psychiatrist at the time said that it was likely a one-time thing. That was nearly 10 years ago."

"Oh, I see."

"They have made it clear that I truly have bipolar disorder and I will take my medication, and I will follow up like they tell me."

"That's good to hear, Diana. When the doctor feels like you can return to work, have him send me a note or letter."

"I think I will need some time to get my feet under me, but I really do want to come back to work."

"That's doable. I'll see you soon." Melanie gave me a hug and said good-bye.

The secret of my mental illness was not a secret anymore. It had been revealed in the most public way possible. In another way, it felt like a weight was lifted. I could be who I was and not have to hide my history any more.

CHAPTER THIRTY-TWO

STARTING OVER

The preparations were made for my discharge from the psychiatric unit. I had requested information on a support group. I had been educated about them when I was in nursing school, and a woman who had a colostomy came to our class and told us about how a support group, for people like her who had colostomies, had helped her adjust to having this change in her life and helped her learn to care for it. She painted the picture of someone who had dealt with this change and been assisted by others.

Kathy, my case manager on the psychiatric unit, located one that met about 35 miles north of Mount Vernon. I made a promise to myself that I would go. This time I went home and dirty dishes didn't bother me. My moods were much more stable, and I knew that I would need to return to work. Part of me was relieved that my job was secure and that my supervisor was fully aware of my status, but part of me began to feel like I wish I could have more time.

My mother and my youngest sister came to see me a day after I got home. It was good to see them, but I asked my mother a question that I was pretty sure I already knew the answer to.

"Mom, I am going to have to go back to work in a couple of weeks. Could you take care of me until then?"

"Well, honey, I'm not sure exactly what to do for you. I'm sorry."

Her answer explained so much to me. She had never known what to do with Dad when his moods were out of control, and she avoided me when I was ill with bipolar disease years ago in Wichita, and now again. I didn't truly want her to care for me, but I did want her to care about me. I wanted her to try to understand me, and comfort me. She gave me a kiss and a hug when she left, and I knew that was the best she could do.

Before I returned to work, I took the trip to my support group meeting. I was surprised to see at least a hundred people at the meeting. They divided the group into 4 groups, so everyone could be heard, and what I heard surprised me.

"I wish I could have a manic event. It would be so nice to have energy like that. I never have that."

"I know what you mean. Manic-Depressives are so lucky. Being depressed is so hard."

I could not believe what I was hearing. Being manic was never a good thing for me. My manic periods had done a great deal of damage to me and my family. I raised my hand to speak.

"I just got out of the hospital after having a manic event. It wasn't fun and it is certainly not something that you should hope for," I said.

"Yea, but you don't know what it is like to be as depressed as I have been," a woman spoke out.

"The name of my disease includes depression. I have depression, also, and it is very painful and exhausting. There is no competition here," I replied.

The exchange continued without any more comments by me. I discovered later that the group was a mix of people who had bipolar disorder and people who had what is known as unipolar depression. Unipolar depressives go from depression to normal mood and then back to depression in a cycle. I did not feel that this group was supportive to my situation, and I decided that for now, I would wait to continue my search for a support group.

I followed up with my outpatient psychiatrist, Dr. T. He was an older gentleman and I would go to his office for a medication check every two weeks. The meetings in the doctor's office were very cut and dried, with standard questions about sleep, energy levels, side effect questions, and mood. I also continued to meet with a counselor, Dr. E., every two weeks. He noticed that I was having periods of feeling down and that every time I would see Dr. E., I would be in either a hypomanic or in a depressed mood. The fluctuation made it hard to keep up with work and home. When my mood was hy-

262 | DIANA DODDS

pomanic, I had to focus more and try not to become too verbose. When I was depressed, I had to push myself to make it through the day. My moods had become like a living teeter totter.

Dr. E. continued to review the MMPI test that I had taken before my last hospital admission for issues that might still need to be addressed. Along with the coping skills he would have me practice, he included a request to rate my mood each day and bring it with me to my meetings with him. Eventually, he came to the conclusion that there was an underlying metabolic process affecting my mood that was separate from the bipolar disorder. He made a referral for me to see an endocrinologist that he was familiar with, Dr. M.

I wrote up a short history of my experience with bipolar disorder along with a questionnaire that she had me fill out. When I was settled in her exam room, I wondered what she would think of me and my history. To my surprise, she had read my history very thoroughly.

"Diana, I read your history, and I think I know what might be going on here. Let me examine your thyroid. Swallow for me." She felt on either side of my throat as I swallowed.

"I feel the scar tissue from the goiter that you had on the left. I am going to draw some labs and have you come back next week and we will review the results."

When I returned, she explained that I had a disease called Hashamoto's thyroiditis. This was a disease caused by the immune system attacking the thyroid.

She also explained that I had a hormone disorder called Polycystic Ovary Disease, which explained my difficulties with fertility. She drew pictures and explained these in detail for me.

"Diana, your first pregnancy lit the fire for your Hashimoto's disease and that explained why you developed the goiter with lithium. Your thyroid will continue to decline as the body's immune system slowly destroys it. We will start you on thyroid medication and follow up with you. I think you will find that this will help your medications to work more effectively."

She was very correct about the thyroid medication helping regulate my moods. They evened out and my life at work and home became much better. Soon, I was able to discontinue seeing Dr. E. My follow up with Dr. T. was decreased to every month and I was faithful in taking my medications.

I heard from Dr. M. that she was going to do a class for physicians at our hospital on hormone disorders that mimicked mental illnesses on one afternoon that I had an appointment with Dr. T. in the morning. Little did I know what that particular appointment would turn into. As I sat down with Dr. T. for my usual medication check, the conversation did not go as it had in the past.

"I want to talk with you today about a way to cure your bipolar disorder," Dr. T. said. I had been told so many times that there was no cure, and so I was surprised at his statement.

"I am going to tear down your personality and put it back together even better than it was before."

I liked my personality and I had no desire to let him reconstruct me. This continued for over an hour as he told me the way he would do this. All that he said seemed to say that I was so damaged that I needed to be rebuilt. I stared at the floor as I began to feel lower and lower. I was overcome with a sense of hopelessness. Never before had a doctor treated my illness as a personality defect. At the end of the meeting, I was having persistent thoughts of committing suicide. My vision blurred with tears as I drove away from his office. I came to a place in the road where I could choose to turn onto the interstate and go to Deception Pass Bridge and throw myself off, or go and listen to Dr. M.'s lecture. I chose to go to her lecture, and to change psychiatrists.

At the lecture, I learned how many hormone disorders could mimic mental illness. I knew that damage to the brain could mimic mental illness as well. I took the opportunity after the lecture to pose the question that had brought me there.

"Dr. M. do you think that my bipolar symptoms might have been caused by my hormone disorders?"

"Diana, I have corrected the thyroid that would have contributed to your symptoms, so the symptoms you have had are not from that, but keeping the thyroid in good control will make it easier. I'm sorry."

"I know, I was just hoping."

I had not bought what Dr. T. was selling to me about being cured of this disease. I knew that it was a chronic condition, and I would have to learn to live with it. This was the first step on a new road.

CHAPTER THIRTY-THREE

WALKING THE ROAD

My husband, Mark, helped me locate another psychiatrist. Dr. J. was kind and our opening conversation included how I felt about Dr. T.'s therapy. I was interviewing her to see if she would be the one to help me. She agreed that she did not know of a cure for this mental illness. It is very hard to accept a life-long illness if you aren't receiving consistent information. She also agreed that I did not need to break down my personality. Starting with a new psychiatrist can be very difficult. You have to tell your story all over again, and develop a level of trust that allows them to help you. This is one of the greatest fears that psychiatric patients have. That relationship is so important and you open yourself up to this person, and no one wants to start over.

Shortly after starting my therapy with Dr. J., I was contacted by a woman who was president of the area NAMI group (National Alliance for the Mentally Ill). She had heard about me from the support group I had attended right after my hospital discharge. She had received funding for establishment of a new support group, which would be occuring in my area. She introduced me to two other women who had bipolar disorder. The three of us eventually started a group that met two times a month. A gentleman joined us, and we met for over a year with just the four of us. After a while, we were getting tired of the same folks, so one night, one of the women and I asked our husbands to attend. It was then that I got a whole new perspective on my disorder.

Mark shared his story of tearing down our son's crib, after he had admitted me to the hospital for my first manic event. He explained how his heart was breaking as his life was turned upside down, and how uncertain his and his son's future had become. His story hit me like a tsunami wave. How self-centered I had been all this time, thinking that this illness only affected me. No longer could I think about allowing my moods to get out of control without thinking of the damage I was doing to those who loved me. That was the moment when I determined that I would do my very upmost to stay stable for their sakes as much as mine.

Over the next twenty years, this support group grew, but the idea of having those with the disorder along with our important others proved to be an effective way for both sides of the situation to examine how their behaviors affected the others. I learned new things every time we met, and I was challenged to educate myself, so as a nurse I could help explain the new therapies as well as trying to lead the group into self-discovery.

One night, as the group of twenty people met, I noticed a young woman come in, and as she sat down, her gaze immediately went to the floor. I recognized that look as one that indicated that she was struggling with an internal demon. There was an air of sadness about her.

"I would like all the new folks here tonight to look around the room. We have people here with mental illness and those who are support people to a mentally ill person. Can you tell who is mentally ill?" I paused as they looked about the room and most of them shook their heads no.

"This is to show you that you do not have a large M on your forehead."

This usually lowered the fears that people had of sharing their life stories with others, but this evening the young woman did not raise her eyes, but I saw tears forming in them. As other members of the group shared their experiences and questions were asked and answered and encouragement given, I began to see her lift her head.

"Would you like to share this evening?" I asked her. "

Yes, I would. This is very hard for me. I am a professor at a college. I became manic, and I thought I was Jesus Christ. I dressed in white robes and walked around. I can't go back there."

"That's nothing, I thought I was God," a man spoke up across the room.

"I was a prophet of God," I told the group. "Has anyone else had a delusion of grandeur?"

Hands shot up around the room as one after another shared their own experience. At this time, I saw a smile cross the woman's face for the first time that evening. She finally knew that she was not alone. This was the purpose of a support group.

During the twenty years of leading this group, I saw parents who were stunned by their child's first manic event. The danger of having a child soon to be considered legally as an adult meant that they had to act quickly to get them into therapy and on medications while they still had leverage as parents. The grief that they felt, when seeing their child's future change before their eyes, struck home for me. My oldest son, Patrick began to change emotionally while still in sixth grade. There were more changes as he went from symptoms of obsessive-compulsive disorder, which was almost at a level requiring hospitalization, to later the development of deep depression which did cause hospitalization. The fight to keep him afloat was rewarded one night, when I got to see him cross the stage and receive his high school diploma. His high school counsellor had followed him from eighth grade on, and she gave him a huge hug on the stage. She was one of the few people there who understood what his journey had been. Later in his life, he would have a manic break. My fears of passing on this disease were confirmed. There was a certain amount of guilt, but then again, I had given him blue eyes as well. It was not a choice that I had consciously made.

Now, I was not only a support group leader, but wrote class material to help people to understand ways to manage their illness. I explained what triggers were and helped people identify theirs as I also identified my own. We discussed how to manage triggers with coping skills. I taught them to monitor their moods daily and explained the beginning symptoms of the disease all the way up to crisis symptoms. We then devised individualized plans for their particular symptoms. I had gleaned these ideas from many textbooks, and I taught the class asking only that they pay for their notebooks. I taught free of charge. It helped my self-esteem and it helped them. I had to limit my involvement as I had promised Kathy on the psych unit at Skagit. I learned over time the wisdom of limiting stimulation from multiple activities and also the most difficult thing of all for me: putting myself first. This realization came over time, as I came to understand that if I didn't take care of myself, I couldn't help anyone else or protect my family from the rages of my illness.

Over the years of my nursing career, I observed professional nurses and physicians that uttered comments about patients with mental illness which showed an underlying bigotry. One prime example was a physician who felt a patient who was schizophrenic should be "do not resuscitate" because of his mental illness. The patient's physical issues did not put him at risk for a cardiac or respiratory arrest. One nurse referred to the patients on a medical floor with a mental illness as "them". I would sit in a meeting that occurs from one shift to the next about the patient's status called "report" and hear nurses speak, not always as bigots, but out of ignorance of the reality of these diseases. It occurred to me that these beliefs were set in stone in this minority of health care providers.

One day I approached a colleague of my husband, who worked as a psychiatric nurse and also as a nurse educator.

"Flora, I have an idea that might be beneficial to your student nurses."

"Oh, what do you have in mind, Diana?"

"Well, as you know I work with student nurses on the medical/pediatric floor all the time. They don't know that I am bipolar. I would like to come and tell them my story as a mental patient. I think I can give them a perspective on a functional bipolar person, before their ideas are set in stone."

"I think that is a great idea. We will set you up as a guest speaker for our psychiatric rotation."

The response from the students proceeded the same way each time. They would be surprised to see Mark and I each time we came to speak. They had no idea why I was there and then I would tell my story. After the class, I would open up the time to questions. Almost every time, one or two students would ask questions about people they knew or who were in their family struggling with mental illness. Bipolar illness affects 1% of the general population. That means 1 in every 100 people. All mental illnesses put together show that 1 in 5 people will experience mental illness in their life time. Essentially, every family has someone. That raises that ongoing question. Why is this such a secret?

As time passed, celebrities began to reveal their mental health problems. They challenged the stigma. More information became available in the media. I attended a national convention for the organization NDMDA (National Depressive and Manic-Depressive Association) in Chicago, which was organized and run by people with both depression and bipolar disorder. I attended lectures and then during a break, I found a board to communicate with other members. I asked if there were other members with health care careers. I met two physicians, a medical social worker, and a nurse. They all were mentally ill, but managed their illnesses and were able to work in their fields. As time went by, I wrote to them, and followed their struggles as I shared my own. At one of my support group meetings, a nurse I had known for years came in and we were both surprised by the other. After that I realized that you could not truly know who was ill in the public around you, unless they were in the throes of the worst symptoms. In the final analysis, what seemed to be a terrible event where the worst of my mental illness became evident to everyone I worked around, had turned out to be a release from the secrets of the past.

*Mark and Diana on Mark's graduation from Wesley
School of Nursing*

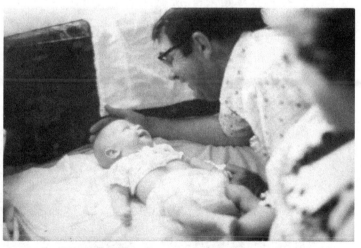

Grandpa Virgil and Grandma Elva with Patrick

Mark and Patrick play in the backyard

Diana reading to Patrick

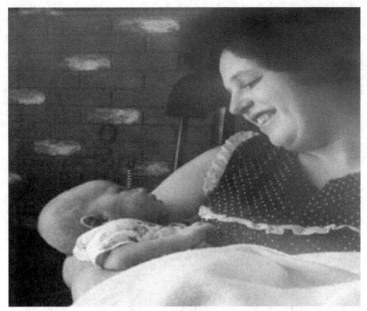

Diana and baby Jacob

Diana with Jacob after a hard day of play

I LEAVE YOU WITH THIS

If there is a theme that threads its way through my story, it is that families have secrets. For every secret a family has, there is a reason, which can be just as interesting as the secret itself.

Mental illness had become a skeleton in the closet, which had ramifications in my life. Perhaps, I would have been more aware of the potential for mental illness had I known the truth. When my Aunt Marie shared her history of electroshock treatments for severe depression, it was like Aladdin opening the cave. The fear of disclosure was so great that she had not even shared this history with her children. I saw my father's behavior in a new and different light. My mother confessed that she had a cousin who committed suicide. The scales fell off my eyes. My best guess for the deep level of secrecy my parents and their extended families had achieved seemed to be summed up with one word: eugenics. Eugenics could simply be explained as breeding. Human beings had been breeding their domesticated animals into all different sizes and colors for centuries. Why not people?

Eugenics laws started in the state of Indiana in 1907. These laws evolved over time and they existed in 32 states in the United States. Some of these laws remained into the 21st century. (1). The idea was that your genetic make-up determined your life. They failed to take into consideration that mutations occur regardless of efforts to breed out a certain item in the genetic make-up of our children. They discounted initiative, the ability to learn, and no effort was made to find a different path. They published their ideas as scientific facts and used such vehicles as state and county fairs, and various publications to push these ideas on the general public. Even baby contests were used to push the idea of superior genetics. What parent wouldn't want to be considered superior to other parents having children?

These ideas got translated into eugenics laws, which also led to mandatory sterilization of certain "less fit" individuals. (2) In case this sounds familiar then you are aware of eugenics as it existed in Germany and all the countries they annexed. In fact, Charles Dight from the Minnesota Eugenics Society wrote a letter of admiration to Hitler. (2) One of the groups seen as needing elimination of course were the mentally ill. Because of the widespread belief in eugenics, families started keeping secrets out of fear, and shame.

That unspoken sense of shame was passed onto me, without my conscious choice or consideration. Eugenics has served to cause stigma, or by another word, bigotry. That unconscious sense of shame is what can develop into something I call self-stigma. Self-stigma leads to self-sabotage. That sense of shame stands like a great wall between those who are ill with mental conditions and the help they most desperately need. Not only does it prevent the ill from accepting help, but it also interferes with support from family and friends.

Part of the help that a person should receive when they begin to have symptoms should work as health care works in any other sickness. Diagnosis should proceed as a matter of elimination of illnesses that are not the cause of symptoms. There are illnesses that mimic bipolar disorder. One of those illnesses that mimics bipolar disorder has to do with abnormally high or low thyroid hormone. In my case, I was eventually screened by an endocrinologist (someone who specializes in hormone disorders). She found that I had Hashamoto's thyroiditis as well as primary hypothyroidism. The thyroid problems that I had when taking lithium (the goiter I developed), could be explained by these findings. This thyroid dysfunction contributed to the depth of my major depression after my first manic episode.

When a psychiatrist sets about diagnosing a person for bipolar disorder, they need to eliminate other medical conditions that could be creating the symptoms. Some of these medical conditions include: reactions to medications such as steroids, delirium which can be caused by severe medical illnesses such as infections, ADHD, substance abuse such as cocaine which mimics mania, or the use of depressants such as alcohol that lead to depressive symptoms. This is not an exclusive list, but rather a word of caution about this diagnosis.

If those other options are not eliminated, how can one know for sure they are bipolar? I don't mean that a person should avoid getting a mental health diagnosis, but rather that a person should be treated for what is actually wrong.

How then does the diagnosis happen after other causes are eliminated? A set of symptoms, over a set length of time, have been refined into a book which psychiatrists use to reach a diagnosis, The Diagnostic and Statistical Manual of Mental Disorders or DSM. The most recent edition of this manual at the time of writing is the DSM 5, published in 2013. There are different forms of bipolar disorder. I have described two different diagnoses depending on the symptoms at the time. My first hospitalizations were for Bipolar I, and my second stint 10 years later was Bipolar Mixed. The severity of symptoms may change the diagnosis from one time to the next. At this point in time, there are no blood tests or scans that lead to this diagnosis. Blood tests, scans, and other tests are used to eliminate possible other medical diagnoses and when eliminated, the DSM offers the diagnostic criteria.

The first DSM was put together in 1952. The most recent revision done by the American Psychiatric Association was 2013. These revisions make the diagnosis even more defined and tend to eliminate possible cultural bias. It is not the perfect world we would like, but it is far superior to all that went before. Bipolar disorder has a way of declaring its existence as it did in my case. Sooner or later the symptoms appear. (3)

CRITERIA FOR MIXED MOOD

1. The criteria are met for both a manic episode and for a major depressive episode every day during at least a one-week period. This is like a blend of both moods. Example would be crying one minute and later singing songs at the top of your voice.

2. The mood disturbance is sufficiently severe to cause marked impairment in occupational functioning or in usual social activities or relationships with others, or to necessitate hospitalization to prevent harm to self or others, or there are psychotic features.

3. The symptoms are not caused by another health problem or by substance abuse.

CRITERIA FOR MANIC EPISODE

An abnormal elevated, irritable, and expansive mood. Expansive refers to a belief in one's power and wealth, accompanied by a feeling of well-being that are not based in reality. During the mood disturbance, (which must last at least one week) 3 or more of the following symptoms have continued:

1. Inflated self-esteem (above normal or reality). Grandiosity. Example: "I am the savior" or "I can do

surgery" (when you have not had the proper training).

2. More talkative than usual. The feeling of needing to talk as though there was a pressure to talk that you cannot resist. As it worsens it may be nonstop.

3. Decreased need for sleep. For example: feels rested after 3 hours of sleep or does not sleep at all.

4. Racing thoughts. So many thoughts that come so rapidly that it appears that the person is jumping from one idea to another but it is because they cannot verbalize fast enough to say all the ideas that are going through their minds. This is called Flight of Ideas.

5. Distractibility. (Attention is too easily drawn to unimportant or irrelevant external stimuli) Example would be walking away to look at something in the middle of someone talking to you.

6. Increased involvement either socially, at work, or at school, or agitation. An example would be a sudden increase in projects which there usually is not adequate time to do. Usually leads to over-commitment that the person may not actually be able to sustain.

7. Excessive involvement in pleasurable activities that have a high potential for painful consequences such as unrestrained buying sprees, sexual indiscretion, foolish business investments, reckless driving, or daredevil stunts.

CRITERIA FOR MAJOR DEPRESSIVE EPISODE

Five (or more) of the following symptoms have been present during the same 2-week period and represent a change from previous functioning, at least one of the symptoms is either (1) depressed mood or (2) loss of interest or pleasure.

Note: Do not include symptoms that are clearly due to a general medical condition or delusions or hallucinations that do not fit the particular mood. Example might be a hallucination that is pleasurable.

1. Sad or empty feeling or depressed mood most of the day, nearly every day, as indicated by either the person's description or an observation made by others (such as they are tearful more often than normal). Note: in children and adolescents it can be irritable mood.
2. Markedly decreased interest or pleasure in all, or almost all, activities most of the day, nearly every day (as indicated by either by the person's description or observation made by others).
3. Significant weight loss (when not purposefully dieting) or weight gain (for example: a change of more than 5% of body weight in a month), or decrease in appetite nearly every day. Note: In children, consider failure to make expected weight gains.
4. 4. Difficulty sleeping or sleeping too much. This would be like early morning awakening or inability to get to sleep or sleeping for more than normal

length (more than 12 hours) or even around the clock.

5. The person describes feelings of restlessness or feelings of being slowed down or it is observed by others, nearly every day. More reliable if expressed by outside observers.

6. Fatigue or loss of energy nearly every day.

7. Feelings of worthlessness or excessive or inappropriate guilt (which may be delusional) nearly every day (not merely guilty feelings about being sick).

8. Decreased ability to concentrate, or has difficulty making decisions, nearly every day (either by the patient's account or by observations made by others).

9. Recurrent thoughts of death (nor fear of dying), recurrent suicidal ideas without a specific plan, or a suicide attempt or specific plan for committing suicide.

THINGS THAT WOULD MEAN THAT DEPRESSION WOULD NOT BE THE DIAGNOSIS

1. The symptoms cannot meet the criteria for mixed mood.

There is something that psychiatrists call the kindling effect. A person is born with a genetic predisposition for bipolar disease. A predisposition can be thought of as the kindling you might use to start a fire. It is not a fire yet, but it has the potential to be. Then stressors occur in your life, some good and some bad, but people with a bipolar pre-disposition have a lower level of tolerance for stress. Everyone has stressors in their life, and you can push anyone hard enough to produce a psychotic break, but people with a bipolar pre-disposition will reach that psychotic break much sooner. Once the fire of stress ignites that kindling, it never goes out. (4)

My fire started after an emergency C-section and two months of sleepless nights with my first child. Before that child's birth was years of living with my father, the loss of a boyfriend that I thought I loved, and finding a friend who had committed suicide. The lack of sleep became a "red flag on the play" in the rest of my life, because it could bring back a manic event. (5)

There are differences in severity with bipolar disorder. I was fortunate to have ten years of relative stability after my first two hospitalizations for mania in Wichita, Kansas. I was also very fortunate that the disease did not surface until after I had accomplished my education as an RN, although people with bipolar disorder can achieve levels of education when dealing with their symptoms. Some people with this disease have more extreme symptoms more often. You cannot compare one person with the disease to another, because people are different in personality and knowledge base with the disease, and the severity may differ.

Research has shown that an individual with un-medicated bipolar disorder will have increasing frequency of mood swings and more severe symptoms. Medicated disease still has mood swings, but they are less severe and less frequent which makes them more manageable. (6)

So what does a sufferer with this disease do with the mood swings that continue after medication? Coping skills are the answer to that question. In my story, my counsellor taught me how to decrease stressful triggers that I had in my life at the time, such as the constant questioning by my father-in-law. Other mental health professionals have taught me other strategies over the years. I also sought to educate myself about my disease and found that there were workbooks with step-by-step directions in identifying triggers and strategies for myself. Those books also taught me to identify my own personal disease changes as it progressed from mild to crisis, and helped me develop strategies for all of them including building my own crisis plan, which included an agreement with my husband about his place in that plan and what I wanted in my care. Primarily, I had an ongoing fear of having my civil rights taken away as they were in Wichita. (7), (8).

As a health care provider (RN), I was aware of the side effects of the drugs that I took for my disease. I knew that they could affect major organ systems such as my liver and my bone marrow, which creates the blood cells that we need for oxygen transport throughout the body, cells that fight infections, and cells that allow our blood to clot. The liver alone has 13 major functions in the body that we can't live without. Unfortunately, we have to advocate for ourselves and remind our physicians of the importance of blood tests that monitor those areas affected.

DIABETES

1. Chronic physical illness.
2. Caused by malfunction in insulin-producing cells of the pancreas, which is an organ of the body.
3. Requires careful monitoring of diet, blood sugar, and periodic monitoring of other major organs.
4. Improved control of the illness with exercise unless it becomes excessive.
5. Requires weight loss and diet control, oral medications to stimulate insulin-producing cells to make more insulin, medications to make it easier for insulin to enter the cell, or replacement insulin.
6. Needs careful follow up with a doctor to prevent long-term effects on the patient which will affect loved ones.
7. Beneficial to have a crisis plan.

MENTAL ILLNESS

1. Chronic physical illness.
2. Caused by malfunction in the neurotransmitter producing cells of different parts of the brain, which is an organ of the body.
3. Requires careful monitoring of mood, behavior, thought process, and periodic monitoring of other

major organs that may be affected by the medicines used to control the illness.

4. Improved control with exercise unless it becomes excessive.
5. Requires monitoring of mood, mentation, and to adjust medications as necessary to stimulate or control neurotransmitter production. It requires control of triggers, monitor of sleep-wake patterns, develop and use support systems.
6. Needs careful follow up with a doctor to prevent long lasting effects on a patient and loved ones.
7. Beneficial to have a crisis plan.

This brings us full circle to the origin of this book, secrets, and fears of passing on this disorder from generation to generation. Double blind twin studies have shown bipolar disorder to be highly heritable. There is no absolute in genetics, however. I made a decision to have a second child after knowing I was bipolar. It was a risk, which might have caused my son to face this very challenging disease. My oldest son did develop bipolar disorder.

My takeaway from being a medical health professional (RN, BSN), a person with mental illness, and having family with mental illness, is that education and support are critical. I helped start a support group for the mentally ill in my area, and ran it for twenty years. I encourage my son to attend support groups. The broader your support system, the more stable you can be. Starting and staying on medications with adjustments as your body changes is critical. Having counseling to help to deal with life's stresses is important. Identifying your triggers and developing strategies is something that a counsellor can help you with, but you can also seek to educate yourself about strategies. Knowing your own personal progression of symptoms from mild to crisis and having a plan to deal with them to try to limit that progression is something that is extremely helpful. This requires monitoring your moods daily, by being self-aware. Sleep is absolutely critical. Too little sleep (less than 8 hours) can lead to mania. Too much sleep (more than 10 hours) can lead to depression.

It is very important to limit the activities that you become involved with. Hypomania gives a bipolar person increased energy, acute perspective, and a desire to become involved in too many activities. Allowing that hypomanic energy to get away from you leads to the more severe symptoms as I discovered in my hospitalization in Mount Vernon. The lesson of limiting one's self to 3 activities at most was very hard for someone who had a deep desire to help others, but I learned that taking care of myself came first so that I would not drag my family through more hospital stays. I used to tell people in my support group that they should not see these things as limiting, but instead as one might see ditches on either side of the road. If you go in the ditch you don't go anywhere, but if you allow those limits, you can go anywhere you want. I also had to learn that to be perfect is not possible, and only leads to stress that you give yourself needlessly.

One of the coping skills that comes up frequently in my memoir is that music helps me handle my moods. Sometimes it has to do with the lyrics that speak to my heart as they did with John Denver's song "I Want to Live". That song helped keep me from giving into suicidal thoughts. Other times I am inspired by the music alone. I find that violin music speaks in a way that words cannot. When I was a nurse and I was having a busy day, and I needed to speed up my level of work, I would hum "Camp Town Races". When I was feeling overly energized as you do as you are becoming hypomanic, I would look for quiet music that I could lie down and listen to with my eyes closed. When I was fighting the loss of energy that comes with depression, I would look for music that would make me move, that had a good beat.

I discovered that, though bipolar disorder is considered a disorder of mood, that it was also a disorder of energy. When the mood is rising into the manic region, the energy also rises. That is why a manic person can get by with little or no sleep and not feel tired. That might sound appealing until you learn that before people could be treated for mania, they used to die from exhaustion. Depressive moods, on the other hand, are low energy. I have often described depression as like walking through molasses.

My faith in God has been a critical part of my mental health. In situations when I stood alone against my disease, I was not really alone. I learned that there is no place, as a physical place, or a space that is an emotional place, that God cannot be with me. When my disease created circumstances that caused me regret and sadness, God's forgiveness was automatic as He understood that an illness caused those behaviors. I also learned that though God's forgiveness is given so readily, forgiving yourself is much harder. My faith also helped me to see a purpose in suffering. I learned empathy, patience, and the desire to stand for those who could not stand for themselves.

Whatever you may choose regarding having children when you are bipolar, the risk of passing on the disease is many times greater than if you did not have the disease. In my case, no one that had actually been diagnosed with bipolar disorder existed in my family to my knowledge, but I now have no doubt that my father and my aunt had a serious mood disorder. It does not matter whether you are a female or male parent. There is a way forward if you choose to have a child, but it is a difficult road for you and especially for your child, if they develop the disease. The book written by researcher Kay Redfield Jamison, "Touched with Fire", discusses the many creative bipolar people throughout history. She also states that some bipolar poeple are not creative. She does question if in the future genes could be altered to prevent bipolar disorder, that we may find we are throwing out the baby with the bath water. (9)

This book is meant as food for thought and your conclusions are your own. My and my family's story with mood disorders have given me these insights. I know now, most assuredly that secrets such as mental illness need to come out in the light.

RESOURCES:

1. Paul A. Lombardo, *Three Generations No Imbeciles: Eugenics, the Supreme Court, and Buck v. Bell* (Baltimore, Maryland: The John Hopkins University Press, 2008) 294.

2. Paul A. Lombardo, *A Century of Eugenics in America: From the Indiana Experiment to the Human Genome Era* (Bloomington, Indiana: Indiana University Press, 2011) 80,121.

3. American Psychiatric Association, *Diagnostic and Statistical Manuel of Mental Illness 5th Ed.* (Washington, D.C. and London, England: American Psychiatric Publishing, 2013) 123-154.

4. Rachel E. Bender and Lauren B. Alloy "Life Stress and Kindling in Bipolar Disorder: Review of the Evidence and Integration with Emerging Biopsychosocial Theories," (*Clinical Psychology Review*, April 3), 2011, 383-398.

5. Sharma V., "Role of Sleep Loss in the Causation of Puerperal," (*Medical Hypothesis* 2003, October), 477-487.

6. Freddrick K. Godwin and Kay Redfield Jamison, *Manic-Depressive Illness*, (New York, New York: Oxford University Press, 1990) 408.
7. Mary Ellen Copeland, M.S., M.A., *Living Without Depression and Manic Depression 10th edition*, (New Harbinger Press Inc., 1994).
8. Mary Ellen Copeland, M.S., M.A., *Winning Against Relapse* (New Harbinger Publications Inc. 1999).
9. Kay Redfield Jamison, *Touched With Fire* (New York, New York: The Free Press, 1993) 240-260.

ABOUT THE AUTHOR

photo by Christine Campbell

Diana Dodds was born and raised in Northwest Kansas. Her life was not unique but she went into the world with the desire to make a way in it. She took her background in hospital work to lead her into nursing. In the process of getting that education, she also sought her other life goals including marriage and children. Life had other ideas about how those goals would be played out. Mental illness crashed into this life much as the Titanic did into the ice berg. Her background in health care shines a light on these experiences and helps those who are not acquainted with the reality of mental illness to glimpse it. How psychological events impact us have everything to do with how we see ourselves and how others in our lives see it.

CPSIA information can be obtained
at www.ICGtesting.com
Printed in the USA
LVHW022258120819
627343LV00010B/573